Reflections of the Other:

BEING BLACK IN GERMANY

Ethel Morgan Smith

Ethel Morgan Smith

Nov 2012

For the Bridgeport Library,

what a wonderful place

for my book! Thank you!

ISBN: 1-4699-8455-5
ISBN-13: 978-1-4699-8455-1

In memory of my mother

Maudie Mae Baker

October 1921-December 2005

Other Mothers

Mary Emma Bruce

August 1910-Sept 2010

Sheila Briggs Fitzgerald

April 1921-March 2005

Yolande Cornelia Watson Giovanni

January 1919-June 2005

Harriet Goldstein

March 1919-December 2004

Black writers of whatever quality, who step outside the pale of what black writers are supposed to write about, or who black writers are supposed to be, are condemned to silence in black literary circles that are as total and as destructive as any imposed by racism.

Audre Lorde

Contents

Preface by Nikki Giovanni

We are a restless nation whether driven by explorers seeking gold or the fountain of youth; whether by the slave trade giving birth to the Industrial Age; no matter that rotting potatoes started the Irish immigration or that World War I stopped it. We are a nation in movement—the Great Migration seeking relief from the terrorism of the KKK bringing their help, their hope, their promise of a new land or the soldiers bringing their blues and jazz to Europe. We move from Cakewalk to Break dancing seeking something new, something safe, something warm.

Reflections is a woman's journey. Mrs. Darwin stayed at home while Charles discovered finches with different bills; Mrs. Shakleton stayed behind while Ernest sought his ice. Penelope, for that matter, waited for Ulysses. Women wait. But Ethel Morgan Smith travels. Pioneers, which should be verb not a noun, continue to explore the physical, metaphysical, emotional unknowns. And this modern voyager shares an encounter with a great though troubled people. We all are beneficiaries of her *Reflections*. We travel first with our hearts. This is a good map.

Introduction

What was I, a Black American woman, doing in one of the most racist countries in the world? Or I had been told. *Reflections* is a vivid and engaging account of my everyday life as an expatriate in German culture chronicling my exchanges and interactions with scholars, diplomats, students, friends, and lovers during 1997/98. This work depicts a natural tension between old and new, reverence and innovation, and tells a story that is at once timeless and immediate.

Germany is not known as a place that called out to African Americans like Paris, but I felt seduced by the fact that I could experience myself without the limitations of race – or so I thought. Is it possible not to be who one has always been? By involving the reader in my day-to-day life, *Reflections* draws a personal portrait of a Black American woman in a country that professes not to be racist, even though racism kept finding me. This work bears witness to my journey from an encounter with neo-Nazi skinheads to a love story in a village of lilacs.

Although this work is about my personal experience, it is designed and rooted in my knowledge and experience of African American literature, culture, and history. In 1954 James Baldwin wrote in his introduction to *Nobody Knows My Name,* "In America, the color of my skin had stood between myself and me; in Europe, that barrier was down. Nothing is more desirable than to be released from an affliction, but nothing is more frightening than to be divested of a crutch. It turned out that the question of who, I was, was not solved because I had removed myself from the social forces... these forces had become interior, and I had dragged them across the ocean with me. The question of who I was has at last become a personal question, and the answer was to be found in me."

Nearly 50 years later, I found myself faced with the same question: *Who Am I?* A peculiar question for Black Americans. In my own country, race has always described and therefore defined me, first and foremost. Was it possible to shed my black skin? If so, who would I find underneath?

Like other Americans, especially Black Americans, we are defined by our history. But I came to appreciate the manner in which I adapted to German life. I was offered an opportunity to experience racial malaise that was different, but no less insoluble, than racial conflict in my own country. I was well aware that Germans weren't without their racial prejudices. But, as a privileged guest, I was protected from their racism. Instead, German racism and xenophobia seemed directed toward Greeks, Italians, and Turks, who had come to Germany after World War II as *Gastarbeiters,* guest workers.

Reflections will be of interest to Germans and non-Germans who may be concerned with a unique perspective. Reflections will serve as a relevant contribution to the efforts of those who seek to promote racial healing not just in Germany or America, but in the human heart.

Ethel Morgan Smith

January 2012

Chapter 1

DREAMING IN GERMAN

Dreams are illusions from the book
your soul is writing about you.

Marsha Norman

I love Germany, especially its beauty and order. It's an old world that is marked by modern scars with mystery and darkness. But it is the people who became my friends that I love most. When I was a Fulbright scholar at the Universität Tübingen, I had the good fortune to interact and observe Germans as colleagues, friends, students, and lovers. I had no agenda other than being away from home, where I felt my goodwill had worn about as thin as that of West Germany toward the former East. The West had given until their hearts and Deutsch Marks could give no more, according to my students. Upon my arrival the West was close to wishing the wall could be re-erected. Looking closer, I found new anxieties, like globalization and feminism challenging Germans' realities and traditions.

I thought about feminism a lot in my new world, which rarely crossed my mind at home, even though I taught in a department with only one female in the rank of professor, no female chair of the department during my tenure, and male professors who almost always received awards when students voted.

When my son Marcus and I lived in Atlanta, I was active in the women's movement in the late 1970s and early 1980s. It gave me a social life outside of my son's needs and my many unfulfilling jobs. I gave up causes to go to graduate school to become a writer and professor. In Germany, I never saw female professors unless I was lecturing in Berlin, Bonn, Frankfurt, Hamburg, Kiel, or Stuttgart. When I did meet one, she usually had no children. It was too difficult to manage childcare and a career, I was told.

In spite of progressive pregnancy leave policies and the Green Party making feminism one of its central issues, the German professors with whom I spent time believed there was a backlash among more conservative forces, who still believed that raising children is a full-time job and that at least one parent, namely the mother, should forego working outside of the home to raise their children in a healthy and responsible manner.

Being one of those women who had returned to college for graduate work at age thirty-seven, I didn't have to concern myself with childcare as a professor. My son was a college student when I accepted a tenure track position at West Virginia University. At the time of my Fulbright fellowship, I was four years into the process of tenure and promotion.

Gray is a color I had come to know well in West Virginia. Most days, especially in the winters, I felt like I was being held hostage by the bleakness. Living in the hollows of 'little sky country' made me feel like I could almost touch it from my front porch. Rain pours more than 55 inches a year on Morgantown, 19 inches more than in Seattle. Even when sunshine is forecasted, it doesn't rise much above the mountains.

Before moving to Morgantown, I lived in Roanoke, Virginia, where I was a graduate student at Hollins University. I still miss the beauty and drama of the Blue Ridge Mountains. It never occurred to me how culturally different West Virginia would be from other places I had lived. Since Morgantown is in the northern panhandle of the state, I assumed it would have more in common with Pennsylvania, but the culture is only specific to itself, neither North nor South. Even though West Virginia has some of the ugliest elements of the South – pickup trucks, Confederate flags, and guns, of course – the mountain people are more concerned with 'insiders and outsiders,' which often meant natives against the University, or the other way around, depending on your position. Like any other native people, West Virginians have a history of living off the land, but they tend to believe that right has been taken away by 'outsiders.'

I ached to add elements of my past life in Roanoke and Atlanta to West Virginia. Soon after moving to Morgantown, I telephoned Habitat for Humanity, where I had volunteered for years before. I waited three months before anyone returned my call. Finally, the pleasant young woman explained that they were in the process of re-organizing and would call me back. I never heard from them again. I tried again to become involved with the community by joining a hiking group. It was designed around age, which I quickly realized was going to be a problem. My age group hiked for less than an hour at Cooper's Rock. The group was more interested in eating than walking. I then teamed up with a younger group; they were so disorganized I put hiking aside.

Though hiking was a disaster, I did strike luck with a tennis group. Finally, I had something to look forward to other than work. I didn't want to be one of those women who put all of my energy and effort into work, with nothing left for myself. My goal was to use something I never owned — freedom, which meant living a balanced life.

Even though Morgantown had an African American female mayor in 1993 when I moved here, seldom did I see Black folks, since the state has only about 2% African Americans. Later, I met four African American female professors from the history, foreign language, the creative arts departments, and the law school. All were assistant professors, except one who had sued the University for tenure. She was awarded tenure, but she was never promoted to the rank associate. That's how the story was repeated to me.

I rented a house near the University in the Woodburn neighborhood, surrounded by semi-college students and young families with children. It was a nice area, but nothing like the neighborhood of South Park I was shown during my interview process. My rent with an option to buy was $450 a month, plus utilities. The house offered no privacy, which a writer needs. Since the house was close to the street, I was always afraid for my cat, Brandon. Someone lived on each side of me, and behind my house was a rented guesthouse. My house, which had long suffered damage from earlier college student renters, needed too much work that required money and skills. Since I had neither, I only lived at Monongalia Avenue for one year before I bought a much nicer house in the same neighborhood.

During the one year in the rented house, I did everything possible within my means to make it a home. I painted, ripped up old, nasty carpet, and sanded and refinished the downstairs floors. I was glad to leave the house, even though the $3,000 that I had invested in it was never reimbursed. I felt it had been a worthwhile investment. That hadn't been the dream I had in mind when I moved to West Virginia in my new position.

My new house sits on a hill, a blue Cape Cod from 1910. Despite its age, it was solid, in good condition after the improvements made prior to selling. I was able to relax about Brandon the cat, whom my son brought home from school in his book bag fifteen years earlier. We took the tiny, two-week old black cat to the vet, where we were informed that Brandon would be more appropriate than Brandy, the name Marcus had chosen. The cat used to ball up and lay under the reading lamp on my night table. Brandon, our black and talkative cat with large blue eyes, was a wonderful addition to our small family.

Once in my new house, I hosted dinner parties, baby showers, potluck suppers, and other gala festivities. I assumed my social invitations would be reciprocated, but it seldom happened. I was rarely invited to parties or anyone's home. Watching *Martha Stewart Living* on television offered me hope that I could create an artistic and joyous space in my new home. Martha was helpful in everything, providing me with tips on creating fabulous dinner parties to demonstrating how to plant a garden. I even learned how to tape her shows. My social life had previously always been active, but living in West Virginia made it clear that a change had come. There wouldn't be progressive potluck suppers anymore. Socializing often came in the form of taking job candidates and guest speakers out to dinner.

Marcus was always afraid for me living in West Virginia alone. On rare occasions, I was scared too. He taped his voice as the greeting on my answering machine. One day, a colleague said she had tried to call me. When I asked her why she hadn't left a message, she said it was because the voice on my machine was that of a white man from New England. When I told her it was my son's voice, she asked if my son was white. I told her he couldn't be white since I am African American; she never spoke to me again.

Some of my new colleagues were what they called eccentric. One puzzled me until I mentioned it to my office neighbor. I asked why Marion, the petite professor nearing retirement, was friendly at times yet at other times she wouldn't say a word to me. I was informed of the office joke: that Marion only spoke to people who wore purple, or at least some hue of that shade.

I saw fewer and fewer Black folks as I settled into my new world. Traveling to Washington, DC and Pittsburgh grew exhausting after a while. If I didn't grade papers each weekend, I would get behind on my work. I taught five classes a year, and since the Department of English is so service oriented, the work is endless. Writing letters for students, advising students on an informal basis, and not to mention the most significant category of my profile: research. If you don't publish, you're not awarded tenure, which means you're fired.

I started watching *The Cosby Show*. I hadn't seen a lot of the show when it first aired since I was a busy graduate student at the time, but it was a lifeline in West Virginia, my only encounter with Black folks those first few years living there. Other than teaching, working on my house and watching *The Cosby Show*, I started to ask myself, was this all there was? I had done *it*, succeeded when the odds and even some friends had been against me. Sixteen years after completing my undergraduate degree, I had returned to graduate school. Most important, I had raised my son on my own. Not only that, but I had raised him well; he was excelling in graduate school at Harvard Divinity. Now where were those friends who had convinced me that there would be men at WVU? After all, it was a university town, complete with schools of law, medicine, dentistry, engineering, and all those other male-dominated fields. This was supposed to be not just my life, but my dream life. Why did it feel so empty?

My neighbors are mostly nice and considerate on Louise Avenue, a ten-minute walk from the downtown campus.

Only one of them gave me problems, a man obsessed with my catalpa tree that sways towards his property, dropping leaves onto his treeless backyard. Trees are a big part of my landscape – two huge golden maples, one box elder, five lilac shrubs and a grape arbor. My house sits on a piece of land that, like much of West Virginia, is 'almost heaven.'

During my second year of blissful living, someone banged on my backdoor before 7:00 am on a Saturday morning. I assumed something was wrong since anyone who knows me also knows that I am not a morning person, especially on the weekends. I put on my robe and rushed downstairs. Through the window, I saw my neighbor, a portly bald stump of a man standing at my backdoor. I knew he was there with a purpose; no one comes to my house by accident, since you'd have to open my gate before entering.

"What can I help you with?" I didn't open my backdoor, hoping I sounded as annoyed as I was.

"The other folks who lived here said I could cut down that tree." He pointed to my gracious catalpa tree. "The leaves fall on my property. And that ain't right."

"They don't live here anymore. I own the property now, and no trees will be cut down." With that, I walked away from the door, too awake and annoyed to go back to bed. I brewed a pot of coffee and turned on the radio to hear the news. After reading the newspaper, I went upstairs to work. My office feels like being in a tree house. Sitting at my computer I looked out on the September sun shimmering on the golden maple tree leaves and noticed that the lilacs needed to be cut back; they hadn't bloomed last spring.

Normally they bloomed around the same time as the wisteria that crawls up my garage. Sometimes I called my yard where Faulkner meets Whitman.

Further up the hill I saw a dirty white house. The run-down hut didn't look so bad on the days where the West Virginia sky was clouded over, but that morning, with a perfect pristine blue sky above, the house looked gray. A soft wind picked up; I heard the flapping of my neighbor's flags. There are many flags in my neighborhood, mostly on the houses of World War II veterans and Republicans. The bountiful Hosta leaves were still green. I tried to write.

As much as I loved my new house, it requires a lot of work for a single woman, especially the yard. I didn't worry about the leaves. Once they all fell I would have them raked and taken away. Sometimes winter set in before that happened. Autumn is a short season; the leaves added dramatic decor and beauty to my life. When the cleaning service didn't show up, I could clean my house but not the yard. Anna, a colleague and friend, recommended a former coal miner to help me with my yard. He had taken care of her family's property for years, and I was elated.

At first, Jimmy, the yard person, seemed nice. Despite working deep in the mines for years, he stood tall and erect on my front porch when he arrived for his first day of work. His $17 per hour fee was expensive, but I hadn't been responsible for a yard for more than twenty years. The first time he cut my grass, it looked spectacular, but I couldn't afford to pay him $85 every time. I rationalized; after all, the grass only needed to be tended for a short period in the spring, and since it rained so much in the summer, it would probably be okay.

I telephoned Jimmy when the leaves needed to be raked the next autumn. He came two weeks before Thanksgiving. After he finished raking leaves and cleaning the gutters, he asked if he could borrow $100. I told him that I didn't have that much extra money, but after I paid him in cash, I gave a check for $50. I told him it was a Thanksgiving/Christmas gift, not a loan.

During our Thanksgiving break, I lunched with Anna and told her the story. It occurred to me that we had never discussed how much she paid Jimmy.

"I like his work, but he's too expensive and works very slowly since he's being paid by the hour."

"What do you mean?" Anna asked.

"Seventeen dollars per hour is a lot of money, and it takes him at least five hours to complete the job."

"You pay him seventeen dollars per hour?" Anna put her hand over her mouth.

"That's what he said when I asked him. What do you pay him?"

"Eight dollars."

"You're kidding me, right?"

"Oh, Ethel, I am shocked. I had no idea." Anna shook her head.

"Did he ask to borrow money from you?" I asked.

"Yes."

"Did you give it to him?"

"Fifty dollars. My husband is letting him work it off. And believe me when I say, my husband will be supervising him."

I wasn't hungry anymore; I felt sick to my stomach.

When I told Mother the story later, she was angry too. "Who ever heard of payin' that kinda money for rakin' leaves? Lord. Lord, what de world comin' to. Sounds more like what Auh used to make in a week. Can't believe you throwin' 'way good money like that."

When I arrived in Germany in 1997, I was treated well by my mostly male colleagues, better than at my own University. In West Virginia, my colleagues weren't rude, just not friendly, indifferent most of the time. Rarely did anyone want to discuss anything with me. Most of the time, some wouldn't even say hello unless it was necessary. In Germany, I was sought out for intellectual discussions, opinions, and debates. How the Germans love debates! They were well versed in American literature too. My German colleagues often threw parties in my honor. People were interested in knowing what they could do for me. I received more invitations to give lectures than I could ever accept.

Students weren't coddled like they are at home. No one cared about the students' evaluations, especially the professors, as they were not a criterion for being awarded tenure. This was a relief; I hate student evaluations. Mostly they serve as an opportunity for students to vent and say ridiculous things: "She made us work too hard,"; "What a bitch,"; or "I had a headache all semester from thinking too much."

German students have to keep up with their own *Schienen*, grades. Their graduation or upkeep of it is their responsibility. Europeans don't make such a fuss about graduation as we do in the States. Despite this, students read assigned texts with great interest, contrary to most of my students at home who often acted as if they were doing me a favor when they passed in assignments. In the States, I even had difficulty getting some students to come to my office to take an exam they had missed.

There I was, away from home, teaching at an old university where 500 years ago, two hundred students gathered for the first lecture, the beginning of an unbroken continuity of academic life and work. The early political and social conditions weren't favorable in the small *Swabian* town. Courage for change and the capacity for reform have helped the Universität Tübingen prevail throughout the centuries.

Tübingen is an old city, which first appeared in the *Chronicle of Trier* in 1078. Today it's a name on everyone's lips. In the years between, the decisive word was *attempto*, to dare. This is what made Tübingen what it is — a university town. Though the city is old, Tübingen is dominated by the young. I felt the energy between the virtues of an ancient institution and the promise of youth as I walked the streets where Hegel and Hölderlin had roamed hundreds of years before me. The rhythm of the semesters determines the pace of life in Tübingen, with a population of more than 50,000 natives and more than 20,000 students.

My first stop in Tübingen was when I was on my way to the Universität Kiel, where I was to immerse myself in a six-week German language camp during that golden August of 1997, before classes would begin in October. My host professor Bernd Engler was on holiday but had arranged for his assistant Oliver Scheiding to pick me up at the airport in Stuttgart. I was to stay with Oliver and his young family for a week. His was the first of three different families that I would stay with for a week each until my flat became available. I could have stayed in a guesthouse, but that seemed lonely. Since I was trying to learn about a country whose language and culture were new to me, living with professors seemed like it would be helpful while adjusting.

I had told Oliver over the telephone that I would be the Black woman at the airport with too much luggage. He didn't laugh, but I felt comfortable around him and his wife, with their new baby boy. While staying with them, I slept most of the time. I was exhausted; there had been so much work to do before I left the States, getting my house ready for renters and preparing my office so that other colleagues could use it. No one had helped me, not even Marcus, since he was moving from Cambridge to New York City as I was readying to leave. One of my colleagues in the department told me she didn't have the heart to help me because it would remind her how much she would miss me.

The row of houses along the Neckar River was my first view of Tübingen. I fell in love immediately with the picturesque gables of the stately old houses with their red-tiled roofs. They stood much like a stage set to form a stunning skyline behind the world-famous Hölderlin Tower, a small room with sunlit windows on three sides and a view of the *Neckar* and *Steinlachtal*. Friedrich Hölderlin had lived the last 36 years of his life in that tower, mentally ill but still writing and meditating. The Tower was the home of Zimmer, a family friend of Hölderlin, who admired and cared for him. There Hölderlin wrote the "Poems of the Tower," with the lyrical variations Spring, Summer, Autumn, and Winter, which he identified with imaginary dates and signed with the name Scardanellli. All of his work is in the Tower Museum.

I had never seen a place so magnificent, especially not a place I could call home. I wondered, do people really live here? Or is it all part of a clever museum staging of "the venerable university town"? I was going to love it here; it wasn't possible not to love such a place. Slowly, I learned that it was all real. Only in Tübingen can you hear the lapping of the Neckar's waters against the punts. Tübingen is considered to be a, big little town' with narrow streets. For me, it was the getaway that my soul was crying out for. At home, my time was rocky. Although I had some friends, most were busy with their own families. To keep busy, I traveled a lot along the East coast, but as joyful as it was, I found it was exhausting and expensive.

The Neckar separates the Old City from the southern valley, while the Eberhard Bridge connects it. One side is bounded by the city walls and is popular with theatergoers, or anyone who wants to flirt or read. Going back up the Neckar on a barrage or boat will allow you to enjoy the view of the Neckar hills and the castles. Going down the barrage, you can admire some of the most beautiful houses in the city. I often sat where the watermill once was under ancient trees and watched the water of the flowing river.

Across from the Old City is Neckar Island, located between the river and the navigable canal, and the Neckar and

Alleen bridges. There is no record to show when the avenue of sycamores trees were planted on the island, which is home to the Summer Theater. Everyone frequents the beaches, especially lovers who want to walk and feed the ducks and swans.

The Universität Tübingen has been educating future leaders, the qualified new blood in Baden-Württemberg. Regional importance goes hand in hand with being open to the world. Its excellent international reputation has enabled the Universität to attract a high number of students and visiting scholars from all over the world.

I was anxious and excited to learn about my new world. In its 1997 mission statement, the Universität Tübingen reiterated that commitment to education and to the humanist educational goals and principles formulated by its founder Count Eberhard von Württemberg. According to its literature, "Tübingen has always been aware of its responsibility and seeks to serve the cause of improving the conditions of human life." I felt that the new mission statement was prepared just for my arrival.

New houses for nobles, clergy, respectable personages, and citizens rose on the hills of the Upper City and around City Hall. The Universität shaped the city's appearance into the face of today's city, which took form as the Universität and the Student Residence Hall were built in 1478.

I was astounded and thrilled to learn that such a small city had such a large selection of international film festivals, theaters, a dance theater troupe, famous orchestras, readings, attractive exhibitions, cabarets, and concerts with well-known soloists. The Universität contributes to such attractions, especially the museum in the Hohentübingen Castle. The Universität also owns quite an art collection, accessible to everyone. The scope of the enrichment programs is parallel among German universities.

If my University town had half as much of a cultural life as Tübingen, I wouldn't feel so trapped most of the time. I had expected Morgantown, West Virginia to be similar to Madison, Wisconsin; Chapel Hill, North Carolina; or Ann Arbor, Michigan. I had been dreaming.

The Department of English at West Virginia University was located in Stansbury Hall, housed in the same building as the ROTC and an old gym. My office, like most, had no windows. In the winter, the offices were cold, and in warm weather, hot. I kept a sweater in my desk drawer. Cold air blew out of the vent above my head. I stuffed the vent with old socks. Florescent lights were hard on my eyes. When I stayed in my office for more than three hours, my head hurt and my eyes burned. Everyone complained about the bad air. The OSHA people sent a team out to test the air once; their conclusion was that we should clean our offices more often.

The department seemed to be divided into categories: theory; creative writing; and old people, waiting to retire, who didn't fit into either category. From what I was told, some of my male colleagues had been promoted to the rank of associate by simply stating to the promotion and tenure committee that some publisher had expressed an interest in their work. Although I am a creative writer, I also teach American literature courses: African American, Southern, and Women's literature. I thought it would be a challenge for the department to fit me into a category, but they did: The Lone Black Woman. However, it was surprising to learn that in 1993 only one other African American male had been in a tenure track position in the Department of English at WVU. Further, that one lone Black man had left the tenure track to take a position in the NYC area. During those early days at WVU, I believed I could make a difference by inviting diverse writers and teachers, by teaching African American literature.

Money was complicated at WVU. Faculty members weren't paid during the summer months like I had been at Virginia Tech. I was always trying to plan extra carefully with money. During my first year, I decided to buy airline tickets early for the holidays for Marcus and myself. Across the street from my office was a travel agent. When I walked into the office, I almost turned around and left. Two women sat in front of their desks. They were so obese they could not sit behind their desks. I was pleased that I pulled myself together and didn't walk out. I had never seen anyone so morbidly obese. They weren't friendly; in fact, they didn't even seem interested, which surprised me since I was their only customer during the entire time I was there.

In spite of that experience, I liked the head of the department, who had hired me; everyone else liked him too. I felt like my new career was manageable, and I could build a life in this small and mostly white college town.

Mother couldn't understand why I couldn't teach at Troy State, Alabama State, or even Auburn University. I tried to explain to her that I wanted to be on the East Coast to be closer to Marcus; she couldn't argue with that. At the end of the conversation, she would always ask the same question, *when you coming home?* Alabama would never be my home; it was the place I was born. Home was where I lived my life. I made my home as I lived.

On Halloween of my first year in West Virginia, I walked downstairs for the newspaper. I couldn't open my screen door. Overnight, eight inches of snow had fallen unexpectedly. For the first time in 30 years, the University was closed. I called a neighbor and colleague who told me to make a grocery list; her husband was going to the supermarket in his truck. This would possibly be the last chance for a food run for the next couple of days, even the week.

I graded papers and caught up on my reading as snow fell steady and softly around me. I cooked vegetable soup, baked corn bread, and ate oatmeal for breakfast. I felt like a mountain woman. I was a mountain woman. I thought about inviting friends over, but it occurred to me that I might need the food if snow continued to fall. Daytime television was boring, all soap operas and game shows. I gave my house a thorough cleaning. If I was to live in West Virginia, I would have to learn better coping skills. After the storm, I bought a stereo and three Ella Fitzgerald's CDs, the beginning of my music collection.

It was the language camp at the Universität Kiel that I didn't think I could survive. The only university in the Schleswig-Holstein area of Germany, it is considered the Universität of the Baltic. The city of Kiel is only a ferry ride away from Denmark. It is also the birthplace and former workplace of Max Planck, one of the most important physicists of the 20th century and the founder of Quantum Theory, for which he was awarded the Nobel Prize for physics in 1918.

Kiel is called a special city, with charm that is enhanced by its long tradition as a port and nautical center. Quays are located directly behind the central railroad station, the ferries of the Scandinavian lines docking alongside schooners and cruising ships. The city's annual 'Kieler Woche' is the world's largest sailing festival, which is very much a part of life in Kiel.

My time in Kiel was one of the most painful experiences of my life. No English was spoken in classes since my Russian and Polish teachers didn't speak any. "What a dirty trick," I said the first time I learned how the courses were taught. I was one of the few professors to take the six-week language course. Others were mostly students, young, and white; all had been involved with the German language since high school, through college and family. Many had even majored or minored in German. I had to work hard at seeing my language torture as an opportunity. "I am smart. I can do this," I declared out loud every day before my classes from nine in the morning until three o'clock.

My nights were filled with assignments I didn't often understand. I agreed with Mark Twain's essay, "That Awful German Language." But before Twain wrote his famous essay, Emperor Charles V said, "The German language was only fit for speaking to horses." I knew I was in trouble when

I couldn't roll my Rs. The language is precise and throaty, aggressive, and in your face. It made me feel like I was always fighting.

Prior to this, the only exposure I had to the German language had been through a former German boyfriend, Helmut. I'd met Helmut at a pub in my university town. My colleague and friend, Anna, had invited me to attend because she had promised her German students she would be there. Like me, Anna had been a Fulbright scholar in Tübingen, she enjoyed working with German students. I was dog-tired on that day, but I didn't want to let her down. And since it was my last day of teaching for the week, I could rest later. When we met, Helmut was attending graduate school and teaching at WVU. He was only supposed to be in the States for one year, but after we met, he stayed two. He made it clear from the start that he was always going to go home to his *serious* girlfriend and a family *house*. Through Helmut I grew familiar with some German culture and a bit of the language, but it wasn't much; he was more focused on immersing himself in my culture, not teaching me his own. But I wished I had learned more of the language. Who knew I would need to know German?

Rachel, an architect from Boston, was my only friend in Kiel. We were among the few adults at language camp. I would visit her in Berlin after Kiel, and she would visit me in Tübingen. In Kiel, we walked in the *Volksgarten*, where roses and hydrangeas flourished everywhere and welcomed us with open blooms to the land of old. Although there wasn't the beauty of Tübingen, Kiel had beaches. Twenty minutes from lecture theatres, beaches lined the coastline. Rachel and I went to the beach almost daily. One day, Rachel said something that has stayed with me. "Life is interesting. One day, you've never heard of the Baltic Sea, and the next day, you're swimming in it."

We loved watching families play volleyball in the nude. The Germans seemed more comfortable in their bodies. They didn't appear as obsessed and repressed with sex as Americans; it was more natural, like the human body. I liked this new attitude. I would not have survived without Rachel. We swam with a current of a different history.

But after being in Kiel for six weeks sleeping on beds as hard as cobblestones, with two student roommates who had no idea how to clean or organize, I was thrilled to get back to Tübingen. I found it even more beautiful than I had remembered. Pictures and books don't do justice to the quaint, medieval red-roofed town. The beauty of Tübingen will always make me cry.

But I was puzzled as I listened to Germans in the streets. I could not understand a word they spoke, despite my time studying in Kiel. I continued listening to my language tapes, and my new department even arranged for me to have a television set from the media department. It only had three stations, two of which were the same. I did begin to understand a little of the language from a soap opera, but I felt that I should have been doing better; I'd never worked so hard at anything in my life.

To learn a language you need a buddy, someone equally motivated and easy to be around, just like going to exercise class. I learned about a program at the Universität called *Tandem*, whereby I would work with a German to help improve my language skills, while the German would improve his/her English skills. I signed up. Just when I thought the summer of Tübingen couldn't get any more golden, the program sent me Silvia, a tall, slim, stylish woman with long flowing dark hair and expressive eyes. Actually most of the Germans I encountered in Tübingen were dark, unlike the stereotype most Americans have of Germans being blonde and blue-eyed. I learned later that the Romans had soldiered through the southern part of Germany hundreds of years ago and colorized the population.

Silvia and I hit it off immediately, which surprised me. I had expected someone like the German teachers in Kiel: old, old world and non-English speaking. We devised a system to meet twice a week, once in my office to work with texts, and then in the *Stadt* to shop and socialize. Silvia taught me that learning a language could even be fun, a revelation after my first experience at Universität Kiel. By spending time in the *Stadt*, I learned useful German. My ears ached from listening so hard. Listening is a must in learning a new language. As a southerner, I also had to learn not to smile often. Germans seemed to be a brutish bunch.

When I told Silvia how discouraged I was, she assured me that it was okay. *Swabische* is a particular vernacular, and I didn't need to know it. The "*Swabian* seat of the muses" played a significant role in the state of Württemberg from its beginning, but that wasn't helping me with this most difficult language. Maybe I simply could not do this. Maybe the brain wasn't capable of making such adjustments as learning a new language after the age of 40. Maybe I could.

"Just listen for key words. Listening is the best key," Silvia repeated to me. If you're willing to embrace another language at my age, you must be willing to make a total fool of yourself. I was, but this was a new level of humiliation. Strangers could even laugh and point at me. Every day was a struggle, but like a good German, I soldiered on.

One of the most important words in the German lexicon is *verbot*, to prohibit. Every rule a country could possibly of seemed to be written on everything. The next important word is *verstehen*, to understand, which I often did not, but I used the word combined with *Ich nicht*, I do not.

Without my English/German dictionary, my Bible, even the most basic tasks became a struggle. One day, I needed matches to light candles in my flat. Without a car, my shopping was usually limited to whatever could fit into one bag, the necessities. I dashed to the store for this one item, leaving my dictionary behind without thinking. At language camp, I had learned that the market provides all the information I could possibly need. I thought I could get by on my own. When I didn't see any matches, I asked the grocer. In my desperate state, helpless without my dictionary, I asked in English first. No one understood. Finally, I managed to make due with what I did know: *Feuer Stecken*, fire sticks. The word I was looking for was *Zünd*, but the grocer understood right away and laughed.

After that, every time I went to the market I would say hello to the helpful grocer in German and we would chat about the weather. He would always tell me about the specials of the day in German, which I embraced as a sign of respect. Often when I tried to speak German, the merchants would answer in English. Germans were always looking for ways to practice their English, Silvia told me.

I relished all of my victories with the German language, no matter how small. Soon after my incident with the grocer, I figured out an advertisement for bathroom and kitchen tile on the side of a truck. I felt victorious and humble. It then occurred to me what life was like for the illiterate – hard but bearable.

The Market Place is the entry to the Old City, a reception area, special event location, and a leaving point. For me, it was more – a place for daydreaming and night dreaming. The Market Place in Tübingen is a place to exchange old and new, the home of markets of every kind. When I shopped at the outdoor market, walking around tasting food that was foreign to my tongue, I felt European. The Greek flower ladies who wore black printed headscarves and long black dresses with lots of gold and silver jewelry were my favorites. During the chilly early fall weather, a fire would blaze in the center of the market area and music hung in the crisp air. Often the music was familiar to me — Smokey Robinson and the Miracles piping "I Second That Emotion" or "The Piano Man" by Billy Joel. Sometimes I didn't recognize the tune, but I always felt it.

The only drawback to the market was the time. Merchants arrived at 7 a.m. and only stayed until noon. Not being a morning person, I had a hard time rolling out of bed and down the hill. Typically I arrived an hour before close, when most of the merchants were loading their trucks and were simply not interested in customers. I complained to Bernd Engler, my host professor.

"Why can't they come from 9 to 3, or something more civilized?" He reminded me they had been doing it their way for hundreds of years. And they didn't realize I was not a morning person.

Once the Greek ladies learned I was an American, they grew more curious. Since I bought all of my flowers from them, they would save their best flowers for me. A dozen roses cost about five dollars, a gift I gave myself every Friday. Trying to learn the language was paying off. To me, it's clear who I am. I look and speak Western. Imagine how surprised I was one day when one of the flower ladies thought I was Brazilian; another one said African. That was as far as their imagination could take them. Finally, I told them I was *Amerikanisch*. "*Amerikanisch, Amerikanisch*", the women repeated to each other down the line. They were disappointed when I told them that I didn't know Whoopi Goldberg or Bill Cosby. Their dream was to go to California or Florida where the weather was warm. New York City was too big with too much crime. When they asked where I was from, instead of saying West Virginia, I said Atlanta, knowing that they were more likely to know major cities. They shook their heads like they knew of Atlanta.

I had a life in my new world. With no personal responsibilities, I could just be. But did that mean protecting myself from the Germans? Did I have to? Was it possible to put down my survival defenses? They were not *the* Germans, but people I was getting know and care for. I was feeling the Germans, not just in their space, but in their hearts.

I taught two classes — "The Tradition of Slave Narratives" and "Women Writers of the Harlem Renaissance." My teaching schedule didn't allow me much time for my research, but I wasn't concerned. I shared an office with a more than semi-retired Professor Weber, who only came in on Monday and sometimes Friday afternoons.

I met Silvia in the *Stadt* on those easy Mondays, when I had no plans other than to experience a medieval town. We walked in sunshine and in rain. On our walks I had to remember to look up from our conversations to admire the trestle beams, bow windows and decorations, facades rendered classical by harmonious colors and wood paintings. Sometimes we would stop and examine old tavern signs. Colorful flowers decorated balconies and windows. Silvia spoke passionately about her love for her country's art and artists. She talked about Germany's wounds with great insight toward healing.

Her perception even extended into my life. Silvia believed I could live in Europe, at least part of the time if I wanted, and I could have interesting lovers. I did not have to be afraid of change; I could embrace it. Friday mornings with Silvia in my office, our private language class started with friendly hellos, tea, and texts. I asked questions about how someone had spoken to me or what I had heard spoken and didn't understand. That would set in motion the class for the day.

The small staff of the American Studies program enjoyed those fun Friday classes, too, with our laughter and exclamations ringing throughout the halls. Silvia taught me German with pleasure and passion. I tried to learn her language in that same spirit. One day, we met at my house because Dr. Weber had a meeting in the office. The staff was so disappointed when we didn't show up, leaving the office quiet and without laughter, that one member offered his office to Silvia and me, if we should need it again.

Like spring weeds, my neighbor in West Virginia popped up again, making his unwanted appearance by banging on my backdoor. When I saw him, I didn't answer. He saw me. A few days later, I received a certificated letter telling me he was going to build a fence around his house, and he had spoken to an attorney who had informed him that he could cut my tree down without any further notice, since the previous owners had promised they would cut the tree down.

I had to put an end to the harassment. I sat down in front of my computer and wrote a letter to Mr. & Mrs. Crazy Neighbor, telling them that if they banged on my door one more time, I was going to call the police. In fact, if either set foot on my property, I would call the police. I informed them they had been badly misinformed by their attorney, and if they touched a leaf on my tree, I would sue them for even their dreams. I didn't even need to wait for them to harm my property; I could at that moment sue them for harassment. I sent the letter via certified mail.

They stopped speaking to me, which was more of a blessing than a loss, and the harassment ended. Three years later, Mrs. Crazy Neighbor died. As in life, her death wasn't without drama. At least three times a week, the ambulance pulled into their driveway. Sometimes, late at night, I could hear her from my bedroom window screaming at the ambulance attendants, "You better not drop me. I'll sue you." This went on all summer. One day, I didn't hear her anymore. Then, I saw her obituary in the local newspaper. That night, I lit a candle and listened to Malahia Jackson sing "In The Upper Room" and hoped if my neighbor had any evil spirits they would be buried with her. The neighborhood was exhausted from Mrs. Crazy Neighbor's nightly outbursts. Everyone was sleeping in. I wished her crossing over could've been more peaceful. The soft music from my wind chimes made me forget about her.

I received a fellowship from the Humanities Foundation in Charlottesville, Virginia to work on my book-in-progress for the summer of 1994. Although Virginia was hotter than its neighbor state to the west, I was happy to be back. Though I had never lived in Charlottesville, I had lived near there and knew it well. The old charming town was like a friend welcoming me with both hands. I rented a guesthouse from a widow near the University of Virginia campus. She was lovely but lonely and wanted to talk all the time. I told her that I wrote at night and slept during the day, which took care of the problem.

But the news that summer was not about me or anyone other than the murder of O. J. Simpson's ex-wife, Nicole, and her friend Ronald Goldman. Everyone was glued to their television sets, watching the trial. My landlady had her help, an elderly Black man, transfer one of her televisions to the guesthouse. She and her friends were changing their doctor's appointments so they wouldn't miss a thing about O. J. I could hardly believe that the world seemed to have stopped. Just when I thought it couldn't get more dramatic, there was a car chase with a white Bronco. All of this has become a part of our collective memory.

My friend Kim and her sister Debbie lived in Charlottes-ville, and they helped me with my needs, including finding a woman to braid my hair. I played tennis with a group called "Getting Acquainted with Tennis." I was often invited out to brunch afterwards. It then occurred to me how lonely I was in West Virginia. Rarely did anyone invite me anywhere. Charlottesville felt like Roanoke and Atlanta. If I got bored in Charlottesville, I could drive to Roanoke where there were always welcoming friends.

My WVU colleagues seemed coupled, often with small children. The other parts of their lives didn't seem to extend outside of work. I found no one with whom I could to go to the movies, shop, or just hang out on a regular basis. Occasionally someone would call if her husband went out of town. Week after week, I kept finding myself with no plans and alone. It was clear that Morgantown would be my work place; anything else I needed or wanted had to come from elsewhere.

After I returned from Charlottesville, I was even more determined to have a social life. I wasn't going to sit in my house weekend after weekend. I rethought my rationale for moving to West Virginia, the thinking that the University had medical, law, dental, and pharmacy schools, which would increase my chances of meeting a companion. Despite my appealing qualities – intelligence, looks, personality, and world experience – I was having no luck. None of it mattered. I learned quickly that you must bring what you need with you. That's what most of my colleagues had done.

The Cosby Show became my best friend. Why not? It was funny and entertaining, but most importantly, not insulting to Black folks. In fact, everyone loved the family and wanted to be a part of it. I wished I could have a life like Theo's Professor Grayson, who took Theo's class to Egypt to see King Tut's burial site. I dreamed what it would be like to receive an invitation from one of my students' parents to come to their home for dinner and have intellectual discussions.

The only contact I had with parents was when one called to find out why her son had received an F in my class. I told her that her son had only been to class five times during the semester, and he had not taken any of the exams. "But we paid the money," the parent responded. I told her that was a conversation she should be having with her son. I bet Professor Grayson from *The Cosby Show* didn't receive those kinds of telephone calls. I went home that day and prayed for a repeat of *The Cosby Show* with the episode about Professor Grayson.

The student population was looking more racially diverse by my second year, with more students of color. If I saw an African American student during my first year of teaching at WVU, it would usually be someone from the football team. In my African American literature classes, the few students of color I taught were not just African American – there were a few Caribbean and interracial students, who always wanted to discuss their whiteness and their right to their whiteness. I always wished them well on their journey of identity 'passing.'

The few African students I taught were always angry because someone had mistaken them for an African American. They constantly complained in class that their ancestors had never been slaves, and they didn't appreciate being called "Nigger." I told them, "Welcome to America."

One day after class, one of my better students stopped by my office. In class we had just completed a discussion on the novels *Quicksand* and *Passing* by Nella Larsen, a Harlem Renaissance author.

"What can I do for you?" I always start off asking students that question. It saves time, of which I had little.

"Professor Smith, I'm glad to be taking your class. You see, this is the only chance I've had to learn anything about being interracial."

I was a little surprised since the student was the color of milk chocolate. She looked more like me than white. "I see," nodding for her to continue.

"My mother is white, and my father is Black. He left when I was a baby. It's so awful, Professor Smith." The student cried.

"Where are you from?" I handed her a box of tissue.

"Wheeling," was all that she was able to get out.

"I am so sorry."

"My mother remarried a white man. Now I have a little brother. Everyone in my family is white except me," she said, continuing to cry.

"I see," nodding again for the student to continue.

"What's really bad is that my three uncles are policemen. We eat Sunday dinners together as a family. All they do is say 'Nigger this' and 'Nigger that.' And always ending, 'The world would be so much better without Niggers.' Then they turn to me and say, 'We don't mean you, Gloria.'"

"Do you know any of your father's relatives?"

"Not a one. When I've asked about them, I get the same answer, 'They ain't worth knowin'.' And I never hear from him."

"You're one of my best students. With only a year left, I think you should start applying for graduate schools on the East Coast or West Coast, or any place as far from Wheeling as you can get. You're always talking about wanting to be a psychologist."

"For real?"

"Of course. Being a good student gives you choices. The process is tedious, but it's well worth the effort."

"What about money?"

"I am sure there are fellowships for graduate school, for excellent students like you."

"Thank you."

"You deserve so much better." I hugged my student.

Later at home, I watched one of my favorite episodes of *The Cosby Show*. Denise decides she wants to be a teacher. Grandy, the family matriarch, and a retired schoolteacher, visits the family from Virginia. In the last scene when Mavis Staples sang, "Have a Little Talk With Jesus," and "He'll Answer By and By," I prayed I had given my student the best advice.

The only other time I had given advice to a student was when a white female came into my office to tell me she had a 'thing' for Black men. Her baby's daddy was a Black man, but he was in prison. She was trying to decide whether to tell him about the baby or not. I asked why he was in prison. She said breaking and entering. She and her baby lived with her parents in Cheat Lake. I told her to never tell him.

Another observation I made when I returned from Charlottesville was that many of my colleagues had gained weight. I don't mean ten pounds, but twenty-five to fifty pounds. How could someone put on so much weight so quickly? Would this happen to me? Was the question not "would it happen to me," but "when?" I had never worried about weight until I moved to West Virginia, which has the third highest obesity rating in the country. I bought a stair stepper and used it on the days I didn't play tennis.

West Virginia scared me in other ways, too. I hated going to the grocery store or other routine errands. Too many people were not only morbidly obese, but I hated how they'd stare at me and wouldn't say hello. In the South, everyone says hello, especially if eye contact is made. The only happiness I found outside of work was my house and tennis. Even though the indoor tennis center is a dump, I was thankful there was a place I could play during the long winter months. And once you started to play, you didn't notice that the place was in such disrepair.

A colleague on my floor told me if I placed an extra cable on my stereo I could pick up the Pittsburgh's NPR station, which broadcasted jazz. Our West Virginia station was very local. Sometimes I forgot I was listening to a national broadcast. Once I got involved with the jazz station, I learned more about the music. Even *The Cosby Show* helped. I hadn't realized how music played such a big role on the show. I started to recognize artists like Count Bassie, Little Jimmy Scott, Dinah Washington, and other musicians like James Brown, Nancy Wilson, John Coltrane, and so many others who became part of the show and my life.

Faucets in many houses in Morgantown were installed incorrectly. I assumed that the town had a left-handed plumber who roamed about putting faucets on backward. When I visited a friend's house, I noticed the same thing: H meant cold water and C meant hot water, just like at my house. When I asked about the faucets my friend laughed and laughed even harder at my theory.

The faucets turned out to be the least of my troubles. My beloved department head was stepping down. I was shocked and scared. It had been his vision that had made it possible for the department to have a Creative Writing program. A new chair could turn the life of a newly hired tenure track faculty member upside down. Those who had already secured their tenure position had less reason to worry.

I still couldn't figure out why Silvia needed me for my English skills. Her English was already excellent, and on top of that, she speaks Italian and is learning Greek since her family shares a summerhouse in Lefkas, Greece. Germans often own or have close ties to summerhouses in Italy, Greece, Switzerland, the Rivera, and other exotic places. Silvia and I talked about our children, but our aging parents were a constant on our minds. Silvia's father wasn't well. But most of all we laughed. Everyone knew of our mutual admiration.

One night after midnight, my telephone rang while I was listening to Johnny Hartman massage me into sweet dreams. My first thought was that someone from home had mixed up the time difference, but it was Silvia wanting to know if I would help her write a grant proposal for a position at the University of Oregon's International Program. She apologized for waking me. I told her that I would.

After that telephone call, my recurring nightmare I had about mistaking my trains because I couldn't understand German stopped; no longer would I accidentally end up in Siberia in my sleep. My dreams were always gray, never any color. Gray was the color of my new home in Germany. But I was beginning to feel at home in my in my new world. Langston Hughes had been right, "For Black folks in America, no place is home, therefore, every place is home."

Chapter 2

GRAY ILLUSIONS

Illusions are art, for the feeling person, and
It is by art that we live, if we do.

Elizabeth Bowen

Two days after Silvia and I met for German lessons at my house, I woke to the radio announcing that Frank Sinatra was *Tote*. Though I didn't know the German word, I immediately knew that 'old blue-eyes' was dead. I felt I was going to be dead by the time I learned German. Other than learning to roll your Rs, verbs are key in learning German. I had a new textbook that had 501 verbs. Germans don't use language like Americans: they have one word for a thousand things. For example, we say beautiful, pretty, cute, attractive, grand, magnificent, etc. In German there's just one word and that is *schön*, sometimes *sehr schön*. Silvia was impressed in my analysis of both the German and English languages and thought I was catching on.

Instead of going into the *Stadt* for our usual time together, we lunched at Silvia's house. Her son, Jonas, had been sent home from school because his teacher was sick. Germans didn't have substitute teachers. There was an assumption that a mother would be at home if a child became ill or was sent home for any other reason. He accompanied us for our learning expedition of the day.

My lesson for the day was shopping at the market, by walking around with Silvia and naming all of the fruit and vegetables. *Apfel, Aprikose, Birne, Pflaume, Zitrone, Rohne, Rosenkohl, Salat, und Spargel.* One way of learning the names of food is to take a menu from a restaurant and study it. That's what Rachel and I had done in Kiel at language boot camp, and it was paying off in the market.

The second part of my assignment was to ask the butcher for an order by using numbers. Even something as rudimentary as numbers is drastically different in German: where we say twenty-five, they say the inverse – five and twenty. I had to ask until he understood me.

One day while waiting for the bus, a man came up to me and asked, "*Wie spat ist es?*" I rolled my eyes upward and hunched my shoulders. How was I to know how late he was? Silvia told me later that the man had asked me what time it was. We laughed.

It was not only Silvia's sense of humor that impressed me. Every day she would eat a little chocolate that she kept in her purse. If I had chocolate in my purse, I would gobble it all down immediately, which is the same reason I try to keep small amounts of food in my house. Silvia and her husband Klaus have traveled and worked in the States. Klaus speaks good English, though not as fluently as Silvia. Part of her position at the International Center for Academic

Cooperation, which is a consortium of 19 universities in 10 nations, is international recruitment, mainly in Oregon and California.

I learned from Silvia that when their sons were young, she and a small group of friends had worked out a system for childcare, since there was none in Tübingen. I thought one of them should open up a top-notched childcare center and get rich; after all, there was no competition. The men would adjust since they respected money. While so many American women work because they simply have to. Many would prefer to stay at home. In Germany, a college professor's income and social standing are in the same category as attorneys or physicians in the States. People don't become doctors simply to make money, since they often do not. I wondered what was better: to stay at home because you can and have no power, or work because you have to and also have no power.

I don't know if there are childcare centers today. Like mine, my friends' children are grown.

Before I arrived in Tübingen I knew what my teaching schedule would be. I had proposed to the Council on International Exchange Commission to research the political momentum of Afro Germans. The only Afro German I met was Tina Bach, a student in one of my classes; she was the only person I saw who looked anything like me. Berlin or Cologne would have been better venues to work on such a project. I kept good records about my experience and trusted the writer in me to know that I would have something to write about after my experience.

In the meantime, I wanted to write. Writing is different when you're away, and I couldn't have been more away. Since Germany was in the middle of Europe, I was free to travel and see the new world I had been awarded. About 30 minutes from Stuttgart, many Germans consider Tübingen a gateway to the world.

Early April of 1997, my host professor telephoned me one Friday morning, six months before I was to arrive in Germany. It was 8:00 a.m. for me and 2:00 p.m. for him. "Hallo, this is Bernd Engler, the person you'll be working with in Germany."

"Oh. Good morning." Hoping I didn't sound as sleepy as I was.

"Did I wake you?"

"No. Not at all. You see, I live alone, and you're the first person I've spoken to. That's why I sound sleepy."

He laughed. At least he had a sense of humor. All I'd been told at this point was that Germans were orderly and arrogant. I remembered Helmut as being orderly, but then again, he'd been trying to fit into American culture at the time. I couldn't know what he would have acted like in his home country.

"I am calling to introduce myself and say welcome. I also wanted to see what your needs are with regard to housing."

"I am looking forward to being there. Thank you." He didn't sound German. His accent was only slight, more international. Helmut hadn't sounded German either, unless we got into a fight. What did Germans sound like?

"After this call, we can then communicate via email."

"That would be fine."

"Your needs," he said.

"I need a bathtub."

"Anything else?"

"Sure, but that's a main need."

"What about a kitchen?"

"I figured there would be a kitchen."

He laughed again. Did I have a better sense of humor than I thought? I didn't think asking for a bathtub was such a big deal, at least not laughable.

With that phone call, my life had changed. I would work and live in Germany for a year. I had begun a new chapter in my life, for I was a Fulbright scholar.

My German students were older than my students in the States, thus making it possible for us to become friends. Once they got to know me, they invited me to *Bier Gartens* near the Neckar River, where ancient chestnut, linden, and sycamore trees stood guarding the magnificent medieval town. The German beer was wasted on me. A *Radler*, a drink made up of half lemonade and half beer, was the closest to drinking beer I got. The verb *rad* means to paddle a wheel or a bike. In essence you can drink *Radlers*, and still peddle your bike home or, in my case, walk up the hill.

More than half of my students had studied and/or spent periods of time in the States; as a result, they spoke English well. A handful of them believed that the Queen's English still reigned. They were well read and sophisticated, but they misunderstood some of the nuances in African-American literature. For example, because of anthologies, Alice Walker's "Everyday Use" is one of the most popular American short stories taught in German high schools and universities. In the short story, Walker alludes to quilting as a basis for "high art." Further, during the 1960s she criticized the tendency among some African Americans to give up the names their parents gave them, names which embodied the history of their recent past, for African and Muslim names that did not relate to a single person they knew. Hence, the mother character in "Everyday Use" is amazed that her daughter Dee would give up her birth name for the name Wangero. Dee was the name of her great-grandmother, a woman who had kept her family together against great odds. Wangero might have sounded authentically African, but it had no relationship to a person she knew, nor to the personal history that had sustained her family.

Because of that short story, German students assumed that changing one's name was an African American tradition. I never tell students they are wrong, so with the Germans, I concurred with them to a point. I observed that changing one's name was as American as jazz. I used Cher, Gary Grant, Bob Dylan and Marilyn Monroe to make my point. I talked about how immigrants had come to America and changed their own names in order to become more American. Sometimes the custom agents misspelled names of individuals, and those misspellings were often kept. Alice Walker's short story offered me an opportunity to open up a discussion as to why African Americans had and continue to change their names. This discussion led the class into the institution of slavery.

Later that week, I walked to the *Rathaus*, city hall, to learn about the process Germans had to undergo to change their names. The *Rathaus* is graced with *graffito* paintings on the façade that speak of important men who put their minds and lives at the city's service. I found three paintings most impressive, women representing Justice, Agriculture, and Science that were amiably displayed on the front facade. On the decorated tympanum, the astronomical clock testifies to the mathematician Johannes Stöffler's love for experiments and success. The *Maenad* expresses the importance of grape growing and the wine trade in the region.

I was told that name changing was not encouraged. In fact, Germans offered a list of suggested names to future parents. To change your name, a fee of 1500 DM, about 700 dollars, was imposed, and the person had to write a 1500 word essay expressing why such a name change was necessary. Afterwards, the request had to be approved by a committee. No wonder Germans rarely change their names; it was too complicated.

Bernd Engler told me my classes were full, and the students were excited to begin. I was pleased. "Excited" wasn't language I had ever heard when speaking of students and my classes. He suggested that I not allow anyone else in the class since it was supposed to be a seminar. I listened and thought it wouldn't be a problem. The class already had more than 25 students, which couldn't be much of a seminar. At home I would've simply allowed students in the class who asked on the first day. There would always be students who never showed up, so it balanced out. When Germans signed up for something, though, it was like giving their word – they stuck to it. All students showed up for registered classes. There was no room for extras.

I arrived to my first class a little early and a lot anxious. When I first started my teaching career, I had a recurring dream that I would show up for class on the wrong day, wrong time, or wrong place, and everyone would laugh at me. In Germany, the dreams before my first day were worse; I dreamt that all of my high school classmates spoke German and were laughing at me because I was in the wrong place at the wrong time and couldn't speak German. But in real life on that autumn morning, no one was in the classroom when I arrived. Did I have the right room? I doubled-checked; I was in the right place. After waiting for about ten minutes, I walked upstairs to see what the problem was. Tina, the secretary laughed and then informed me that professors had a 15-minute grace period. I didn't think it was funny since someone should have told me. After that glitch, the first day went well.

The following week an excited American woman showed up in my office wanting to know if I would allow her to audit my "Slave Narrative Tradition" class. I said of course. Then she wanted to chat about where I was from. Where had I gone to school? Did I come from a wealthy family? She was in Germany the typical way, following her husband. They had two precious children and were happy to be raising them out of America, away from consumerism.

When Bernd Engler learned I had allowed an extra student in my class, he stormed into my office and told me I was making a mistake. "That woman is trouble, I promise you that." He paced up and down my office like he was lecturing.

"What kind of trouble?" I was confused and surprised at such a reaction. "Do you know her?"

"No, but if she were in the States, do you think she'd be so interested in you?" He took off his glasses and continued to pace in front of me.

"But I'm not in the States. Maybe she would be nice to me." Plus, I was trying to shed myself of automatic assumptions. Of course, I wouldn't have allowed a woman without credentials into my class, but it was only for auditing. I wouldn't have to read her paper since she probably wouldn't be interested in writing one. I didn't know how else to explain my decision without being rude, so I just listened.

"Mark my words, there's going to be trouble." He put his glasses back on and left my office. Even though I am two years older than my host professor, he was very parental toward me. I thought it was charming, unless I was disagreeing with him.

Two weeks later, classes were in full swing. Students were energetic and asked interesting questions that often had little to do with the texts, but with American culture, like the difference between blue and white-collar jobs. I introduced them to the phrase "pink-collar jobs." Students often stopped by my office, always apologetically. I was pleased in my Athena mood. Students told me that they weren't used to professors holding office hours; they felt lucky when their professors showed up to teach classes.

When I was a graduate student at Hollins University, Professor Lex Allen was the great Shakespearian scholar. I admired him and anyone brave enough to take his class. After I graduated, Professor Allen and his wife, Jo, befriended me. We spent many lovely summer evenings drinking white wine, with him teaching me mythology without trying. All of those years ago I chose Athena, the Greek Goddess of Wisdom and Creativity, as my role model. I chose my profession so that I could have a say in the shaping of young minds, which would have an impact on those young minds beyond the classroom.

In preparation to move to West Virginia, I gave myself the nickname Mountain State Goddess of Wisdom, Warfare, and Handicrafts. Though I am not the favorite daughter of anyone like Zeus nor associated with owl or olive tree, as a Black woman I am always armed. Athena has become a byword for "mentor," wise nurturance. She was a force for civilization that helped to bring the younger, more enlightened Olympian gods to power. I was on a journey of enlightenment and creativity, on my way to a tenure track position.

Soon after I accepted the Assistant Professor position at WVU, I received a telephone call from the director of the Center for Black Culture and Research. He informed me of all the work I could do for him, work for all of the students of color. I pointed out to him that my appointment was in the Department of English, and as soon as I found my way, I would get back to him.

But I did attend a few of the meetings at the Center to see what they were about and if there was a project I could become involved with that would directly benefit students – not sitting in some meeting on some committee deciding how many cookies to buy for a reception. I learned about the Mentor/Mentee Program, whereby I would be assigned to mentor an African American student with a commitment of at least two years. The Center offered training and activities so faculty and student could get to know each other in a productive manner. I signed up to participate. No one called. I assumed because it was one of the most popular programs.

The next semester I volunteered again for the Mentor/Mentee Program. In the meantime, a class action suit for $4,000,000 had been filed against the University by a group of current and former female employees for sexual harassment against the director of The Center for Black Culture. The story captured the front pages of national newspapers. The director resigned as a result of the lawsuit but was awarded a higher position at The University of California at San Diego. At WVU, the provost appointed an acting director.

My dream of following in the footsteps of Athena was fading. I couldn't even find an African American student to mentor. Even more discouraging, one of the two African American students from last semester wrote on her evaluation, "This teacher should be fired for teaching books about homosexuality like James Baldwin's *Giovanni's Room.*" The other one wrote, "She made us think too hard." I knew they had written the evaluations because they had even signed their names. I wondered how Athena would've handled such issues. After all, she was a mediator between conflicting claims, preferring respect, reconciliations, and persuasion to brute force. That was hard; I didn't know if I could do it.

I spent some time talking to two African American students. Both had been excellent students in a former class. I asked them about the role of the Black Center in their lives. If students were involved with the Center, it was because they wanted to travel to Africa, since that was the main focus of the Center. What about African American culture? Mostly African, they repeated.

Finally, the next semester I received a telephone call informing me that I had a student to mentor. Her name was Janie Peyton, a junior majoring in political science. She told me about her plans to go to WVU's School of Law and her dreams to work for Blacks and other poor people in West Virginia. We met once a week and talked about books and current events. I often took her out to dinner. Shopping was always part of our outing since she didn't have a car. I felt like the mythological gods had blessed me. Janie was talkative, intellectually curious, friendly, and funny. Since she had her career already mapped out, we didn't have to spend time talking about that part of her future. I often wondered what she wanted from me since she gave me so much more than I thought I was giving her.

I was feeling wise, powerful, and armed, like a skilled diplomat, a perfect patron for female professors. My dreams were coming true. I even got a new mentee, a male this time. He was busy and doing well; I never saw him. He had a bad habit of not showing up for appointments or calling at the last minute to cancel. If we could ever manage to meet, I thought, maybe I could help him organize his time and teach him some social skills. By mid-term I grew tired and frustrated with my mentee calling at the last minute to cancel his appointment, but I didn't want to act like a parent. He stopped returning my calls, and I never heard from him again.

By my third year in the program, I was assigned another student to mentor, a journalism major. I called the young woman and invited her to lunch. She accepted my invitation. While we made plans, she did not ask but rather informed me that she would have to be picked up. I had learned not to have any expectations. "Wait and get to know the student," I kept repeating to myself. Students weren't as nice as they used to be.

The day of our luncheon the temperature was seven degrees, the coldest day of the year. I cooked homemade vegetable soup, baked corn bread, and prepared a salad to toss later. I hadn't asked the student about her eating preferences but figured a college student would be grateful for any homemade meal. I assumed that if she had food issues, she would've raised them when we spoke. I telephoned her when as I left my house and arrived at her dormitory within the agreed time. After waiting 10 minutes in seven-degree weather, I parked my car and walked in the building. Ten minutes after paging her, she came downstairs and explained her tardiness by stating that she hadn't been able to decide what to wear.

I reminded myself that I was going to be patient. On the way home, I asked her the basic college questions – her major, interests, and career possibilities for summer employment. I tried to engage her about her family, thinking that would be easy and would help her warm up to me. When she didn't, I asked her about her grades. She told me she was going to change her major because all of her professors were racists. I suggested we meet on a weekly basis and develop a study strategy to improve her grades. She laughed.

My mentee also rejected everything I had cooked. She said I should've consulted with her, since she was a picky eater. She was so picky, in fact, that her mother cooks separate means for her. She wanted to know if I had any tuna and white bread. I told her that I didn't eat white bread, but I showed her the pantry. I asked what else she ate. She said Mickey D's and KFC. I asked if she realized how unhealthy that kind of eating was. She said she didn't care, but she had put on twenty pounds since her first year. Maybe you should exercise, I proposed. She admitted that she was basically lazy and just wanted to eat and sleep.

Driving home after dropping off my mentee, it occurred to me that she hadn't asked me one question about my life. If she was going to be in my life, I would try to teach her some manners, though I worried it was too late; she seemed to revel in not knowing. She was only able to talk about herself in terms of what she didn't like. When she said she couldn't wait to get out of school so she could make movies like Spike Lee, I wanted to ask her, "In what world are you dreaming?"

I telephoned two friends who taught at universities and told them about my experience. They offered support and shared some of their similar encounters with students. We agreed that there were problems in the universe. My final call was to my son. I told him that if he ever acted like my mentee, I would knock him into next week. He couldn't stop laughing at me.

I reached out to my mentee, leaving messages on her machine to offer my help with her studies. Midterm exams were coming up, yet she did not return my call. The following week, I called my mentee to see how she had performed on her midterms. "I passed, if that's what you're asking," she replied.

Two weeks later, my mentee called to ask if I would take her and her roommate to the mall. I agreed on the condition that they would spend the first thirty minutes giving me updates on each of their classes. We ate lunch at a restaurant in the mall. I tried to engage them in conversation – the kind of books they liked, how their classes were going, etc. They told me they didn't have time to read, both of them giggling. When they did talk, it was about what they were going to wear to a party later that evening. After lunch, we agreed on a time and place to meet. I read while they shopped. Though they were an hour late, they didn't offer a word of apology or explanation. I drove them to their dormitory in silence, feeling exhausted and depressed. What would my idol Athena do?

The next day I looked forward to a lazy Sunday morning, reading *The New York Times* and drinking coffee in bed. My telephone rang; my mentee told me I had to take her back to the mall so that she could return an item that was too small. I pointed out to her that I was not a taxi service.

Two days before graduation one of my mentees drowned, the one I never met. I read his obit in the newspaper and wept. He accidentally drowned while saving the life of a friend. In a haze, I continued my preparation to travel to Germany for my Fulbright.

I liked German students. They seemed more interesting in learning than grades or receiving a degree, and they helped me to practice my German. I required oral reports so that I could hear their English and correct it, which also improved my German. They liked the concept too. As I grew more confident with the language, I'd practice with them. For example, if another student needed to tell me that the student was sick while I was calling role, I would repeat, "*Sie ist krank*."

All of those days weren't always so golden, thoughs. When students were boring and unimaginative, I felt sick, sick of struggling in a country that lacked spontaneity. Every detail of every German's life seemed so planned. I am as organized as anyone, which was one of the ways I survived in a country whose subtitle is *Ordnung,* the German word for order and discipline. However, I needed to be surprised once in a while. Living every aspect of life with an orderly formula was *langweilig,* boring. My German students told me, "Anything unplanned is unacceptable." My students began to catch onto the system, speaking German with me on a daily basis, and this became another outlet for me to learn German. Silvia was impressed with our method.

Three weeks into my Friday morning class, a group of seven teenagers quietly entered my classroom, punks sporting blue and purple hair with earrings in their noses, lips, and ears. They sat on the floor around the edge of the room. I continued teaching. I wasn't afraid or concerned about the high school teenagers; after all, they were just boys. They never spoke. But my students were on high alert, looking at each other and shaking their heads as they squirmed in their seats.

When the class ended, I walked back up to my office to find Bernd Engler and Horst Tonn waiting for me.

"What's going on?" I asked.

"We heard about the intruders in your class," Bernd Engler said.

"They were just kids. Pretty harmless." I walked to my desk to put my books down.

"How can you be sure?" Horst Tonn asked.

"From their smell, I bet they probably heard about the class after a night of drinking and thought it would be a laugh. They seemed more hungover than anything."

"If they come back, we want you to leave the classroom immediately."

"They're just kids, trying to be cool. If they come back, and I doubt they will, I'll ask them a question about the text. That'll keep them away." I sat down and booted up my computer.

"Please try to be serious," Horst Tonn said.

"If you try not to be so serious." I looked up and smiled.

After they left my office, I had to admit that it felt good to be rescued by the men, even though they hadn't rescued me from anything or anyone. I have no memory of any man trying to save me. Would my colleagues at home have offered me protection? Or would they have said I was overreacting, which was what they typically said when an issue of race came up in the classroom. Could this be feminism? All of this was new to me. At home, when a student threw a chair in my classroom because I asked her when she was going to turn in her work, no one came to my aid. In fact, the head of my department reasoned that my students liked me very much, so therefore what I was claiming couldn't possibly have happened. I stopped talking to my colleagues about racial issues.

The wild-haired teenagers never showed up in my class again. Sometimes I wondered about them. Who were they? Why had they come to my class? What were they trying to prove? All I knew was that I wouldn't be seeking answers from Bernd Engler or Horst Tonn.

Class was moving along well, as we discussed *Incidents in the Life of a Slave Girl* by Harriet Jacobs. One student asked a question that ignited me like a lightning rod: "How can we be sure that there were no happy slaves?" I paused and thought about the question, thought about the student. Frozen in my step, I stood rubbing my chin with my right hand, thinking and rethinking my response. First, I realized the student and I didn't share the same historical reference, and second, I wondered if it was possible to talk about slavery in purely intellectual language. Probably not for me, but there in my classroom, I sensed an opportunity to move closer to that concept; I knew I had to answer carefully. To view one's reality from the reflection of another was as stunning as the question the student had asked.

"No. We cannot be sure, but by the mere fact that human beings were enslaved, their families sold like cattle should answer the question. Perhaps there is a more important question for you: After reading this text, would you want to be a slave?"

"Of course not," the student answered.

"Well, I think that's the answer to your question." The girl's question will always haunt me. But more important, I was able to engage without getting defensive or emotional.

Another student raised his hand. "This has nothing to do with what we've been talking about, but why is abortion such a political issue in America? We Germans don't understand it."

"A big jump," I conceded, "but a good question. It's always in the news. I'm sure you hear about it and must be curious. I don't have any answers for you, but let's try to examine the situation and see what we can come up with. I'll raise some questions, and we can continue the discussion as you research the issue. Before we begin, can someone tell me the law in Germany with regard to abortion?"

"Abortion is a private issue. We, Germans are very practical, and abortion is a practical matter. It's no one's business."

I found it compelling that the students would often refer to themselves as "we, Germans." I am a sixth generation American, but I couldn't imagine saying, "we, Americans," or even, "we, African Americans," for that matter.

"There is probably some ancient law written somewhere, but that does not have anything to do with our lives today," another student continued.

"No one really cares," yet another elaborated.

"I see. Now, a good question to begin: Who's having abortions? That may give us some information," I said.

"The poor," one student said.

"This is where the research is important; it removes faulty assumptions. The hefty price tag for an abortion often rules out the poor. Research! Research." I gave my students some websites to begin their research, starting with The National Organization of Planned Parenthood. I didn't want to give them too much information, just offer them starting points. With that, I dismissed class.

As a student prepared her books to leave, she asked, "What does that have to do with the politics of it?"

"Well, let's examine this further. What are some of the fears of Americans?" I answered, happy to have students who wanted to stay after class to continue a discussion.

"We have no way of knowing that," another student piped up.

"Of course you do. What are some of the fears of Germans? Think especially of the current reunification," I hinted.

A student answered uncertainly, "We want to hold on to what is ours?"

"Which is?" I walked back across the classroom using my hands to make my point, palms toward the sky.

"Our culture. Our language. Our heritage."

"And your identity as Germans. Most groups want to do the same thing – hold on to their shared culture, language, and heritage," I said.

After class, I walked up and down *Wilhelmstrasse* searching for the answers my students wanted. Americans don't feel comfortable talking about abortions, other than to state their position, whether it be pro-life or pro-choice. The "national conversation" gets bogged down too often. Germans seemed more interested in talking about difficult issues in an open and honest format. Even though Germans live with the scars of the Holocaust, most never try to deny it. I would like to hear more conversations at home about how women allow men to make decisions about their bodies. What are some of the deeper ramifications of men making important decisions about women's lives? Men have no way of knowing anything about giving birth, losing babies, or not being able to have babies. History always repeats itself if not corrected. When mostly white men are involved with the rights of others, I sense oppression. As always, I was trying very hard not to impose my views on my students.

The following week we completed *Incidents in the Life of a Slave Girl*. German students didn't like reading so many books but wanted to read each book thoroughly. I was sure reading texts in a language that was not their own had something to do with it, though my students would never admit it.

"Professor Smith, I was thinking of this text in relationship to *The Diary of Anne Frank*."

"That's an excellent comparison. It's one of the most important texts of the slave narratives. One problem in America is that many books like this one didn't have a long enough shelf life to stay in the main stream. Just think about this, Zora Neale Hurston's *Their Eyes Were Watching God* was out of print until Alice Walker made it her responsibility to see that all of Hurston's work stayed in print. My point is that this was what happened to so much of African American literature."

"Are there other questions or comments?" I asked. No one responded. "I am anxious to know what you found in your research."

"I was surprised to learn how many abortions were performed in the States last year," one female student answered.

"Remember, your population is about 80 million and we have more than 250 million individuals; our population is three times the size of Germany's, so the numbers are going to seem higher. But how many abortions did you find?" I asked.

"Last year there were more than a million abortions in America."

"What concerns me is that abortions shouldn't be used for birth control," said a male student.

"What else did you find?" I asked.

"Married women have more abortions than single women," the male student continued.

"That's because they're having more sex." At home my students would have laughed; the Germans didn't. "What else?"

"I see where this is going," said the American woman. "If you're saying what I think you're saying, you're dead wrong." She'd hardly spoken before.

"And what is it that you think I am saying?" I asked.

"That Americans don't want abortions because more white women have them, and opposing abortions is a way of increasing the number of white babies. I am a Christian, and I don't want to see anyone kill babies." The American woman was jumping to conclusions that I had not even considered.

"No one wants to kill babies. I believe we are talking about two different issues: what you believe and the right a woman has over her own body," I said, feeling like I was disappearing.

"We want to keep babies from dying. Too many babies die from abortions," the American woman said.

"You have every right to make a personal decision to not have an abortion, but what we are examining in this class is entirely different. I want you to consider women's rights, whether the government or others have the right to make such a decision for a woman." I tried to steer the discussion back to its intellectual questions.

"You're going to die and go to hell." The American woman flew up and screamed, pointing her finger in my face.

I looked at her straight in the eye. Very slowly I said, "Please leave this room. Now!"

"Don't worry, I am leaving. I am a Christian and have no interest in being around folks like you."

"Please leave this classroom now, or I'll call security to help you." I didn't know if there were such a thing as security, but I was trying to be authoritative. For the first time, I felt like I was at home dealing with a student who had behaved badly. I had no idea what this woman wanted from me, but I didn't have to know to kick her out of my classroom. I wasn't interested in her and wanted her out of my class. She wasn't in America where she could throw her racism around like used textbooks.

I dismissed class, ran to the ladies room, and splashed cold water on my face to help me settle down. In my office I put my head down on my desk, counted to ten, and breathed. I did not cry. "Bitch," I exhaled. Someone knocked on my door. I knew it was Bernd Engler.

"*Kommen, Bitte.*" I sat up and pretended I was reading.

"It's Bernd."

"What can I do for you?"

"I told you she was bad news. She came to my office to report you."

"Bitch."

"I told her we don't have such a system here. She had abused your goodwill, which is not how we treat our guests."

"Are you going to keep telling me that you told me so?"

"No, but I did tell her that I would have never allowed her in the class in the first place."

"Did she leave?"

"Yes, and slammed the door. I heard some language on her way out."

"Crazy bitch!"

"That and more."

"How do you know so much about racism?"

"Once when I was in the States teaching, I was told to teach Chinua Achebe's *When Things Fall Apart*. I did not want to simply because I do not care for the text as a teaching tool. Plus, I do not like being told what I can and cannot teach."

"What happened?"

"I did not teach the text, but I overheard some language."

"That's horrible. I'm sorry."

"Thank you. But I knew that woman was a phony. If she were in the States, she would not speak to you."

"Okay, you were right. Beat me."

"Come down to my office and have a drink. I'll invite Horst and Hartmut. They can tell you some of their stories too."

Chapter 3

REISE

*We must get beyond textbooks, go out
into the bypaths and untrodden depths of
the wildnerness of truth and explore and
tell the world of the glories of our journey.*

John Hope Franklin

Reise is an old German word, meaning to travel. The earlier meaning of the word was "to make a pilgrimage," which I like more. Experiencing an intellectual and spiritual pilgrimage in Germany made me feel like St. Francis of Assisi. I had just finished reading Patricia Hampl's *Virgin Time*. Hampl had followed in the footsteps of St. Francis as he journeyed through Italy. Although I am not Catholic, I felt deeply moved by the experience of being elsewhere.

Germany has more travel agents than other countries, probably because Germans have more money for holidays than the rest of us. Not only that, but living in Germany can be stressful. "Too many rules and regulations; it's hard for us to relax at home," students told me. Travelling to other countries gives Germans a chance to relax. Although I did find living in Germany stressful and frustrating sometimes, which mainly had to do with my language-barrier, I often felt a sense of freedom. I understood the German's need to travel.

Another important German word is *Ordnung*, which is related to their strict adherence to schedules and deadlines. For example, being late is seen as sloppy and a sign of disrespect; more so, it upsets the general order. The best example of *Ordnung* is the German railway system. Trains are known for their punctuality. It is a well-known joke that you can set your watch by the trains' arrival and departure times. If the trains are more than a minute late, Germans complain.

Germans are known to take pride in their efficiency, organization, discipline, cleanliness, and punctuality. All of this allowed me to become involved in German life. I embraced their pride. These are all manifestations of *Ordnung*, which doesn't just mean tidiness, but also that which is proper and correct. No phrase warms the heart of a German like '*Alles in Ordnung*.' When it is said, everything is alright, everything is as it should be. The love of order that I shared with the Germans helped me to appreciate the their culture.

The other phrase which Germans cannot escape from is '*Ordnung muss sein*," order must be. This mantra helps them to manage their lives better. Even the German language is orderly. Though their words may be long and guttural, there are no tricks to pronunciation – what you see is what you get. The value of tidiness can be seen in the clean streets, newly painted houses, and the trash confined strictly to the garbage bins.

As my language skills continued to improve, I was able to communicate enough in German to get by, to travel with a certain amount of ease. But there were larger issues than the language. Late that March, I worried about my upcoming trip to Rostock, formerly East Germany. Since reunification, Rostock had become known for its increased violence from skinheads, who had attacked foreigners, painted swastikas on synagogues, and, worse, beaten some Africans to death. Economic depression and high unemployment were cited as the triggers of the rise in violence. I had reason to be concerned.

In 1992 more than 15,000 people gathered in Rostock to protest against the neo-Nazi violence. Police were attacked with smoke bombs, stones, and bottles. More than 75 individuals were arrested. The protest had come a week after gangs of neo-Nazis stormed and set fire to a hostel for asylum-seekers on a Rostock housing estate. The locals had cheered and applauded as the rioters forced the evacuation of the mainly Vietnamese refugees. More than 200 Romanians who had been camping outside of the hostel were also forced to leave. The police were accused of doing nothing to stop the violence, according to a newspaper article.

This reminded me too much of racial riots of the American South where I grew up. I never encountered any real violence when I was young. The fact that my tiny town had no buses or restaurants helped. Not being able to go into the library was the only way I had been directly affected, but racial fear always hung at the edge of our being.

Mother never allowed us to go into stores that wouldn't let us try on clothes. Rarely did we have a need to go into such stores. If we couldn't sew them, we ordered them by mail order catalogues like Sears and Spiegel. That was what we preferred, no encounters with mean white folks. The insults were inconvenient, but we refused to allow them to further damage our souls.

As remote as the Civil Rights Movement was from my small town in Alabama, we felt some of the impact. Dan Palmer's death was a terrifying awakening for me as a child. Like Dan, my friends and classmates could die at the hands of mean white folks simply for being black. Evil lived among us. Whenever I could I watched Dr. Martin Luther King and other civil rights workers on television, marching and working for equality. My grandmother would turn the television off. "Dat ain't got nothin' to do wit you." I dreamed of being part of the Movement.

Dark clouds began to roll in over our lives the year my classmates and I entered the 10th grade. Dan Palmer, one of my classmates, drowned in Lake Eufaula. His body was found at the edge of the park near the lake. He was the first person in our class to die. There were whispers that he wasn't supposed to be in the park or lake anyhow. Others said his body had been put there. I heard the name of Emmett Till for the first time, not from our parents or preachers, but our teachers.

My entire class participated in Dan Palmer's funeral services. I was one of the flower girls. It was hot and made hotter by the fact that the church was packed. As far as you see was a sea black faces swimming in paper fans. Mourners wiped tears and sweat from their faces with white handkerchiefs. One my classmates sang "Precious Lord." I thought I would never stop crying. After Dan's body was laid to rest, the whispers died.

When I raised my concern about traveling to Rostock with the professor who had invited me, she assured me that I had nothing to be concerned about; after all, we'd be in a group of five at the conference, and there is safety in numbers. Bernd Engler and Horst Tonn agreed with my host professor.

Typical traveling in Germany is via train, but Rostock is too far north. I took a train from Tübingen to Stuttgart. From Stuttgart I flew to Berlin, where I joined my group. Together, we took a train to our final destination. Arriving in the late afternoon as the early spring sun slanted over the *Stadt*, I felt at ease. My fears were subsiding quickly.

The Universität Rostock is even older than Tübingen. In fact, founded in 1419, it is the oldest university in northern Europe. I walked around the cobblestone streets and thought of history. Less than ten years ago this place had been governed in ways that I did not know. What did that mean to me? All of the fears of Hitler and Nazi Germany were upon me. I wondered what I would've felt had I been standing in Ghana in front of the Elmina castle, where Africans had been sold into slavery. I was sure I would have been thinking of my ancestors. But my uneasy thoughts of history seemed out of place on that early spring afternoon. Quickly I became caught up with the sights around me – the people of Rostock and the buildings, white stone with red-tiled roofs.

In the center of the *Stadt* the sound and sight of construction held my attention, the sky clouding from the rising dust. I said a silent prayer to bring healing to the fractured land. I couldn't stop watching the people. I knew they were watching me too. It was not the kind of judging stare that I am used to at home, less intrusive; I was being enjoyed almost. The people of Rostock looked different from the Germans I lived among. Their clothes were worn, their hair uncut, and their mannerisms old-fashioned, even by European standards. The merchants were the nicest I'd encountered anywhere, even in the South and Midwest of the United States, and their English was as clear as the day was sunny.

Our living accommodations were at the resort town of Warnemünde, two train stops from the *Stadt*. The short distance felt like a world apart. Located right on the Baltic Sea, Warnemünde's charm is enhanced by its tradition as a port and nautical center. People wandered from all over the world to holiday at Warnemünde. My friend Rachel from Kiel had been right. "One day, you've never heard of the Baltic Sea, and the next day, you're swimming in it." There I was again on the Baltic Sea, having a really good time. The first night we dined at the *Pension* where we were staying. The delicious seafood and steamed vegetables were nothing like much of the German cuisine I knew. Warm and cozy rooms overflowed with wine and conversation. Someone played the piano. I felt like I was having a holiday.

I began to notice something odd in Rostock – many people were loitering about with seemingly nothing to do except be. Our host professor of American Studies told us that for every one professor who made it back into the system, five did not. Many people as young as 40 would never work again. This boggled my mind since I had only gone to graduate school when I was thirty-seven. America is ahead of the game in this manner. When Germans decided on a career, they did it early and they had to stick to their plan. Otherwise, they wouldn't be looked upon with respect. Changing one's career is about as American as the blues. Even in academics, I don't know many people who haven't changed their careers in one way or another. In fact, the average American professional has changed his or her career at least five to seven times in a lifetime.

I was shocked at the first session of the conference. The American women, my esteemed colleagues, were attacking the former East Germans by criticizing their interest in materialism and consumerism. Even if the panelist thought such, we were guests. I didn't like what I was hearing. No one here consumed more than Americans. And, of course, the former East Germans wanted things they had heard about like televisions, cars, clothes, and all of the other junk people buy. The American women at the conference even attacked the women of the former East for having the right to abortions and not doing anything with it. I felt like I would throw up if I remained in the room. I wanted to scream, "Leave these people alone." Instead, I left the conference and went shopping, and I felt good about it. It was one of the nicest shopping experiences I had ever had. Everyone was gracious and friendly.

I sat outside a cafe and sipped Prosecco. I felt ashamed and embarrassed to be an American. What arrogance. What nerve to come here and criticize a nation so fractured. No one is more materialistic than Americans – we are shallow shopaholics. I was one of five Americans in the group and, of course, the only African American. I wanted to be in Tübingen having a discussion about this with Bernd Engler and Horst Tonn, not living it.

My talk was scheduled for the next day at three in the afternoon. It would be easy since I would read from my book in progress and show slides of the photographs that would be included in the text. They had heard enough criticism from Americans to last the rest of their lives. I would thank them for their hospitality and talk about their spirit of optimism, what a shining example they were for the world. I would try to make up for some of the rudeness that had been bestowed upon them.

When I rejoined my group for dinner, I was determined to be angry, but instead, I was just silent. So was everyone else, even our talkative host. Someone wanted to know how I had spent my time. "I shopped," I answered. Nothing else was said. We finished our meal and walked to the train station like a silent whistle.

I didn't sleep well that night. When I did sleep, I found myself in long detailed dreams about Toni Morrison's new novel *Paradise*, which I was reading. I was a character in the novel, but I couldn't get the author to hear me screaming.

The next morning I woke feeling exhausted and head-achy. I told the group to go ahead – I would sleep in and join them for lunch. I couldn't take another session like the earlier one. My major problem was just a lack of sleep. I set my alarm clock for two hours and dozed off thinking about the novel *Paradise*.

Ten minutes before noon I dressed and walked south toward the train station. The last session of the conference ended at 12:45, and lunch would be served afterwards. I had plenty of time. Feeling better, I forgot about my fear of being in Rostock, my thoughts overcome by the rude Americans instead.

I walked to the *Bahnhof* enjoying the warmth of the early spring sun. The train station wasn't busy, which seemed odd, but since I knew exactly where I was going with my *Bahn Card* and ticket in hand, I wasn't concerned. I had just enough time to look over my notes once more. I felt more pressured giving talks when Americans were present. Walking so fast, I almost didn't see three skinheads standing to the right of the door to the *Bahnhof*. At first they reminded me of the students who had come to my class earlier, but they were older and bigger. I saw big black boots, black clothing, lots of body piercing. I was glad to be wearing sunglasses; they couldn't see how scared I was. As I was about go to the platform, the *Gleis*, I heard some loud talk-ing and recognized the word "Nigger." I was shocked to be hearing such a word. As much as racism was a part of my life at home, no one had ever called me 'Nigger' to my face or in this case to my back. I felt sick to my stomach. The station was empty enough that I could hear the echo of the word. I almost stopped in my tracks, but I told myself to continue walking and look straight ahead. I knew if I stopped, I would say something, and that would be an invitation for them to be in my face.

"Nigger Bitch," I heard. Were they following me? Or were they talking louder? Was anyone else in this damn train station? Don't panic, I kept telling myself. This is a train station at noon. Nothing is going to happen to you. Keep walking.

"Nigger Bitch," "Pig," "Nigger Bitch Pig, go home." They seemed to have spat out the words together. I heard their laughter and the clacking sound of their heavy boots. I had to decide to stay at the *Gleis* or walk back upstairs so I could possibly get out of the train station into the streets.

I knew they were following me; I smelled their hate. Not running, but walking, I felt closed in, and no one else seemed to be around. Three mean men were a lot; they could kill me before someone showed up. Don't panic. You're close to an exit. And you can run. Everything is straight ahead. When I didn't hear their footsteps, I assumed they weren't following me anymore, but I was not going to look back. I ran up the steps, quickly emerging from the station into the street crowded with people. I was sweating and couldn't stop shaking. My heart was pounding too fast. *Breathe. Breathe. Breathe.* Count to ten. I didn't know what to do, but I knew I was not going back into the train station. But I had to get to the conference.

I blew my nose and applied Chap Stick on my nervous lips. I dropped my briefcase. Picked it up and almost ran back to the *Pension*, where I wasn't scared. The skinheads couldn't follow me to the private resort; I would be safe. Maybe I could get taxi into the city for the conference. Before I could think anymore, I was on the porch of the white *Pension* with the hanging red geraniums. We all had a key. I nervously unlocked the door to find that no one was home. What should I do? I went to my room and I took off my clothes, got into bed, and cried myself to sleep. I would not tell Bernd Engler or Horst Tonn about this. Was this feminism? This was when I needed the men to save me, but I didn't want to be treated like a child. Was it possible to have both?

I woke up to the smell of food. At first, I thought I had dreamed about the skinheads, but as I redressed, I realized it had been real. I walked downstairs and told our hostess what had happened. She hugged me.

"Just relax. This is not the way of our people. This should not have happened to you. This new world is hard," she said in a thick accent. She telephoned the conference and explained what had happened. She told me not to worry. After we drank a strong whiskey, I went back to bed and slept through dinner.

The next day the conference participants and I took the train back to Berlin like a quiet procession. Why didn't they have anything to say to me? Couldn't they have expressed some form of empathy? Silence is not empathy. They had been so authoritative earlier, and I needed some of their confidence now. I continued to read *Paradise* while my group remained hushed. If I were white, would they have said anything? The question nagged me.

I was the only member of the group who was flying to Stuttgart, and I was glad to be alone. My packed plane looked like something out of a 1950s movie set. An Asian woman and I were the only females on the plane. Everyone else was dressed in grayish business suits. A man across from me was staring at me. I was used to people looking at me, but something about his stare felt eerie and unnerving. Don't make eye contact with him, I told myself. Just keep reading. The other men were reading their newspapers.

The pilot announced that the plane was going to be 15 minutes late. The men grumbled. Fifteen minutes late, what's the big deal? At home the pilot probably wouldn't have announced such a small delay. I closed my book and shut my eyes. *Paradise* wasn't a book I could pick up and put down. Like all of Toni Morrison's work, it required my total attention. The scene of the skinheads kept replaying in my head. Rather than feeling that the incident had anything to do with me, I felt like I was recounting a scene from a novel or a scary movie.

I heard a moaning sound to my right, almost like a sobbing. I looked over my right shoulder and saw the man who had been staring at me. He was jerking off, right there on the plane at 2:00 in the afternoon. I couldn't believe it. His eyes were closed, and with his briefcase in his lap, he was moving his hands up and down inside of his pants. I thought one of the other men would say something to him soon. There was no way they didn't see what was happening, but they just buried their faces further in their newspapers. How can this be? Who were these Germans? Could I just get home? What kind of men would allow such behavior? I wasn't sure that I could take anymore. Then I got angry. What an asshole. I pushed the button for the flight attendant. By the time she got to me, the man went into some kind of seizure. I thought he was going to die.

An emergency medical team dashed through the aisle. Since I was seated in the aisle, I stood up so the team could get to the man easier. The other men kept reading their newspapers. I heard one say his dinner was going to be late because of this idiot. I didn't believe what I was hearing. Maybe I just didn't understand their German, but then I heard another one confirm what the other one had said, "Mein Abendessen ist spat." God damn them, all they can think about is food, and not even good food at that.

The emergency team treated the crazy man with what appeared to be an oxygen machine and told him he needed further treatment and should get off the plane. The crazy man refused. The businessmen in gray suits continued to whine about their dinner being late. The pilot came back and told the man he had to get off of the plane. The man continued to refuse and started fighting with the pilot. The emergency team took him off of the plane.

Ever so softly, the man who had been sitting next to him made eye contact with me and said, "I'm sorry."

By the time I got home, I ached in places I didn't know could hurt. I had no strength of spirit. My brain was dead, and my heart was hopeless. Even my hair seemed to ache. I couldn't settle down. The man on the plane had been too troubling. How could a plane full of businessmen not say anything to a man jerking off in broad daylight on an airplane? When would they have said anything? What would have been their cutting off point? Would they have said something had I been their wife or daughter?

I drank a half bottle of Chianti and got sick to my stomach. It occurred to me that I hadn't eaten all day. I went to the bathroom and threw up. Soaking in a long hot bath, I couldn't shake image of businessmen with their faces buried in newspapers out of my head. I heard the noise of a different history than my own.

The next day I cancelled my German class. Tired and upset, I slept all day. When I woke, I knew I had to do something, but I didn't know what. Mostly I wanted to talk to my girlfriends at home, but because of the time difference, my urgency would be over when I could reach them. Rachel was back in the States at the time. I felt sad and alone.

I walked to my office early the next morning before Bernd Engler or Horst Tonn arrived. I had to settle down from all that had happened. They would know if something was wrong. I couldn't hide my feelings from them or anyone. I didn't feel comfortable talking to them about the airplane incident, so I talked to Tina, the secretary. She got angry, too, and helped me write a letter of complaint in German to the airlines.

"How dare they," she said. "They should at least reimburse you for the airline ticket. I have never heard of such a thing." We posted the letter.

"Please don't tell Bernd or Horst about this."

"Why?" she asked.

"This is pretty embarrassing," I answered.

"Why should you be embarrassed? You did not do anything wrong. You Americans always blame the woman. The man was a fool, and you are embarrassed. What kind of sense does that make? Is this what American women call feminism?"

She was going to tell them, and I couldn't stop her.

In my Harlem Renaissance class, the German students were struggling with *Their Eyes Were Watching God* by Zora Neale Hurston. The females' attitudes toward Janie, the protagonist, were more severe than the men's.

"I don't understand why Janie couldn't just settle down. Why does she have to roam all over the place," one female student commented, sounding more like her grandmother than a graduate student in her late-twenties.

"She did settle down. She was married to Joe Starks for 20 years." I paused and walked around the classroom. "And they were 20 long years." I wasn't patient with my students. I wanted to ask them what they thought about a man jerking off on an airplane, but I knew that would be unprofessional. And, of course, I didn't want to talk to them about my personal life. My wish was that my students had more vision and imagination. They were too smart to be so predictable and boring. They seemed more frustrating and practical on that day, probably because I was still upset about the man on the plane and the skinheads.

"But it seemed to me she would have been happier if she had settled down. She had been married twice, and in the end to a younger man," another student said.

"How old are you?" I asked the class. I got everything from 25 to 35. "So you've been in love at least once." They laughed.

I walked to the other side of the room. "Well, let me give you a clue when things aren't going well, if you're a woman: when your man brings home a mule for you to plow, it's time to go. We're glad that Janie left Logan. Aren't we?"

"Professor Smith, you have to understand, we are preoccupied with earning a living and settling down."

"Most people have similar concerns. Is there better language we can use other than settling down?" I asked the class.

"Why? It works," a different student said.

"This book is a work of fiction. It allows us to explore, or at least take a look, at our own lives and the lives of those around us."

I walked to the other side of the room and continued, "So my question to you is, what you do after you settle down? Aren't you concerned with your internal life? Your dreams and hopes? Discovering who you are as a person? You can always settle down."

"We want to live the life we know," another student said.

"That's fine," I continued, "but what about the life you don't know? What if the life you know doesn't work? Suppose you're not happy in that life? What about exploring the life you don't know? It sounds to me that you're scared to explore the other." I looked out of the window. The red-tiled roofs reminded me that I was in Europe living in a famous medieval town. I smiled for the first time since my trip away from Tübingen.

"I see your point, but we must be concerned with more practical matters," another student said.

"Well, what value would this text be if Janie stayed married to Joe Starks, if he had lived and they had children and lived unhappily ever after? Literature is about possibilities. Life is more complicated than a fairy tale."

"Point well-taken," another student said.

"Thank you. This is a text with a feminist plotline, raising important questions. What happens when life doesn't work out the way we planned? And believe me, it will happen to you, too. We are not called upon to judge, but to try and understand a different point of view than our own. I realize that the main elements we bring to literature are our own lives, but judging isn't going to get us anywhere. James Baldwin said it best, 'The purpose of all art is to lay bare the questions, which have been hidden by the answers.' In other words, your answers are telling me a lot about who you are." I was disappointed and annoyed that my students weren't reading the text for more profound meaning than their own limited lives. They told me they liked it very much. I felt like I had to work too hard that day.

I learned quickly that life is serious for Germans, and so is everything else. Bernd Engler had told me that even humor is no laughing matter, and if you want to tell a joke, you may want to submit a written application first. I always thought he was joking. Serendipity is not a word in the lexicon of Germans. They disapprove of the irrelevant, the flippant, and the accidental, which Americans are more comfortable with and open to. We are not *Ernsthaft*, serious. It's hardly conceivable and not desirable that a good idea might come about by chance or from someone lacking the proper qualifications. It seemed to me that Germans would prefer to forego a clever invention rather than admit that creativity is a random and chaotic process.

The German poet and historian Johann Christoph Friedrich von Schiller wrote, "Obedience is the first duty." This fits into their sense of order. In their own country, Germans hate breaking rules, which can make it difficult because, as a rule, everything not expressly permitted is prohibited. I remember waiting for a traffic light to change while walking to my office. In a country so ordered, I tried to avoid jaywalking unless it was raining, cold, or I was in a hurry, but I happened to be hurried often. When I did jaywalk, Germans would stare me down. On that particular day, several people were waiting too. No car was in sight or could be heard. Among the group was a nun who finally walked across the street before the light changed. I did the same and laughed out loud. When I looked back, several others had also walked before the light changed. They just needed some leadership.

I had accepted an invitation to speak at a café called *Sarah's* in Stuttgart. Usually when I accepted invitations, the host would ask me to speak on a specific African American writer, book, or my own work, but the host from *Sarah's* had given me no guidelines. I had never spoken at a Café before. My talks had been at high schools, universities, and *Amerika Häuser*.

I arrived early and was given a tour of the huge facility that also housed a library and a resource center upstairs. The organization had received government funding, my hostess told me. It was the biggest crowd I had encountered. They even had an interpreter. I was impressed, but something struck me as different from other talks I had given: only women were present. I had been told that *Sarah's* was progressive. Obviously, I didn't understand the connotation of the word "progressive." They gave me a standing ovation at the end of my talk. I felt relieved, but when it came time for questions and answers, the audience wanted to know why I hadn't talked about Audre Lorde, Tracy Chapman, or Alice Walker. I apologized to them and explained that I wasn't given a specific topic at the time the invitation was extended. Plus, I wanted to tell them that Tracy Chapman was a musician.

Afterwards, they bought me too many drinks. I managed to catch the last train back to Tübingen in need of a real holiday.

The next day, my friend Rachel called from Berlin. From the tone of her voice, I knew to ask if she was having a bad German day, our code language for needing a break. "I am having a bad German week." We laughed.

I told her what had happened in Rostock. She said I should have called her in the States. Talking about it out loud to someone who cared made me feel better.

"Why don't you come to Tübingen? We could go to Zürich or Strasbourg for the day. Both are about a three-hour train ride, and we could take the last train back around midnight." She agreed. I like Strasbourg the most of all the cities that were within a day's trip to Tübingen. It was the city of languages, the old friendly city on the hill. Once German, it was now French. Due to its history, you can hear French, German, English, and a plethora of other languages just by walking down the street. We could have also gone to Baden-Baden. Zürich is beautiful, but the Swiss are just Germans, only richer. I still traveled there often with hopes of spotting Tina Turner at the *Bahnhof*. It is known to be one of her favorite hangouts.

A few minutes later, Silvia called, giving me an idea and motivating me to do something different. I was going to have a ladies' luncheon. Finally my friends would meet. I would also invite Lucy Engler, my host professor's wife, and couple of other women I had met. Lucy had been a gracious host to me when I had stayed with her family for my first week in Germany, and we had become friends from going to aerobics together every Saturday morning.

The Greek women were surprised and impressed when I arrived at the market before 8:00 am the next day. I told them I was having a party. "Party, good for you," one said. They had saved peach colored tea roses. Along with the roses, I gave myself the gift of luxurious bath products in scents of lavender, rosemary, and eucalyptus on my pilgrimage.

For my ladies luncheon, I shopped for green, red, yellow, and orange peppers, which were more expensive than meat. I would sauté the peppers with red onions, capers, and garlic – perfect to serve over pasta. Capers, I had learned from the Greek women, could spice up almost any dish. We would drink Pinot Grigio. Silvia would bring chocolate for dessert.

I set my table with blue and white linens. White lit candles glowed over yellow and blue flowered plates I had lugged from Portugal the past summer. The peach roses looked perfect on the table. I bought two dozen and had cut a few short for the centerpiece. The others I placed on the living room coffee table.

I felt genuinely good, the best since Rostock. I listened to Sarah Vaughn sing "September Song" as I prepared for my friends' visit. Spring had finally arrived in Tübingen, and my friends and I welcomed it with white wine and fine dining. What had happened to me in Berlin and Rostock had passed from fear and reality to experience and finally to memory.

My days were organized around music. On Saturdays I listened to classical music, especially Bach's Brandenburg Concertos. Numbers three and four are my favorites. On Sundays I listened to gospel. During the rest of the week, it was all jazz. The day of the luncheon was a jazz day. I felt like James Baldwin must have when he was in Switzerland finishing his first novel, *Go Tell it on the Mountain*, while listening to Bessie Smith and Fats Waller. During my year in Germany, I listened to a lot of Bessie Smith, especially "Downhearted Blues." Eva Cassidy, Ella Fitzgerald, Aretha Franklin, Peggy Lee, Nina Simone, Dinah Washington, and Nancy Wilson also kept me good company.

Silvia loves Lauryn Hill, especially "Mr. Intentional" and "Freedom Time." We listened to Ella Fitzgerald scat, Nina Simone sass, and the savory smooth voice of Nancy Wilson. We ate and laughed like we had known each other all of our lives. I told them about *Sarah's* Café. We laughed some more. Our lunch eased into a lazy evening.

The next day Rachel and I didn't feel like going anywhere. We slept in. When we did finally get up, we lounged about with coffee, toast, and fruit. Finally we walked down the hill to my office, where I introduced her to Bernd Engler and Horst Tonn. As an independent Fulbright scholar, Rachel wasn't associated with a university as a faculty member. She reminded me how fortunate I was to have such a supportive community. I knew it. When Rachel went back to Berlin, I felt a little lonely but happy.

In my "Slave Narrative Traditions" class we were discussing Toni Morrison's *Tar Baby*, one of my favorites to teach. It's a cold text with light, darkness, danger and so much sugar: perfectly written. Gloria Naylor's *Linden Hills* works the same.

I was surprised at how much the female students liked the character, Son, who is supposed to be the predator. "A ragged, starving, African American man who breaks into the house," Jadine, another character in the piece, describes Son. "He is the kind of black man she had dreaded since childhood: uneducated, violent, and contemptuous of her privilege." Yet, despite this, my female students were salivating over Son.

"You understand he is supposed to be the bad guy?" I asked.

"*Yesss*," said one female student. The others laughed. The males were quiet for once.

"But he sounds so delicious," said another student.

"Professor Smith, we don't understand America's racism."

"Racism doesn't just belong to America. You have yours, too. Racism is as old as the world."

"Why should it matter if a person of a different race marries a person of another race?" another student asked.

"Have you ever dated from another race? And if so, how did your parents feel about it?" The room was silent for a long time.

"Professor Smith, race is an 18 to 19th century construct."

"I was expanding the definition to include practice."

"I see," the student answered. He looked like he didn't believe me, but I didn't care.

"But you're telling me that your racism ain't like my racism." I paced as I pointed to the student and then to myself.

"Well, yes," said another student.

"Racism has the same impact everywhere: oppression for all involved, even the oppressor," I said.

"He's just trying to explain our ideas," said another student.

"So, if I tell you that I hate white Americans, especially those of the American South, because of slavery, then is that enough of a reason to be racist?"

"No, but it explains it," the same student responded.

"The only explanation for racism is that it's wrong and no one has a right to it." I raised my hands to the sky.

"That's in theory, but life is more complicated than that," said a male student.

"You say that to me, an heir of slavery? I am not going to let you get away with that. If anything, you people started a lot of this. Ask yourself what was Hitler's goal." It was the first time I had mentioned Hitler in Germany. "While you're at it, ask yourself, how do you, as a nation, treat the Turks, Greeks, and, Italians, who've been here for generations but can only be a real German citizen through blood?"

"That's different," the same student said.

"How?" I asked.

"We're offering you explanations. But what you want is emotional ramifications," the student said.

"You're right, but I can't see how you can have one without the other," I said.

"Plus, we did them a favor by inviting them here to work," another student said.

"The Turkish taxi driver who picks me up at the train station thinks he has paid and repaid that debt. Is that what you would have said to the character Stamp Paid in *Beloved*? Is this what you would have said to James Baldwin when he said, 'To have been where we were, to have paid the price we have paid, to have survived, and to have shaken up the world the way we have is a rare journey'?" I paced up and down the floor, shaking my hands up and down.

"It's just different in this country."

"How is your country so different from other countries?" I found myself defending America or perhaps explaining. I was surprised and impressed with myself. My German students, especially the males, thought they had good excuses for their "isms." No effective professor would pass up the opportunity to challenge such ideology.

I was more concerned about my female students, who seemed less enthusiastic about their future. They appeared to want to get on with marriage, babies, keeping a spotless house, cooking heavy meals, and then looking forward to caring for an elder parent or grandparent. The most imagination they showed in their careers was being teachers. After all, it paid well and allowed for lots of holidays, but most important, it was a very secure position. I couldn't get any more information from them with regard to what they really wanted. I didn't feel like an American, a female, or an African American. I felt like a teacher trying to get the best out of my students, and they were fighting me all the way.

I still needed a holiday. Other than language camp and traveling around lecturing, I hadn't had a real holiday since I had met my Australian friends in Portugal. Even that turned out to be stressful. Dreaming of that holiday had gotten me through language boot camp. I took ten days off during the middle of the six-week session.

On a soft Saturday morning in September, I took a bus from the Universität Kiel to the train station, then to Hamburg, where I flew to Frankfurt and from there continued to Lisbon. I couldn't have survived language boot camp without the break. When I returned to Kiel, I would only have two weeks left. My German classes weren't as painful as they had been. I was making progress; the shape of the language had begun to form in my mind, although speaking the language proved to be most difficult. I had not spoken English until I arrived in Lisbon.

At the airport I happily bought magazines and newspapers. We were encouraged not to read English while taking

German classes, but I indulged in the light English reading. I had forgotten how much I missed reading. I had forgotten how much I missed English. I did bring some German assignments too. I was instructed to keep a journal in German. Though I knew I wouldn't be doing that, I would practice German and study the assignments my instructors had given me so I could keep up with the class. When I returned to Kiel, I would have to speak to the class in German about how I had spent my holiday.

My Aussie friends, the Martins, had invited me to join them to share a villa in Sintra, right outside of Lisbon. Our friendship had started when our sons were roommates at a Connecticut boarding school in the late 1980s, and we remained friends.

Marlene, the mother of my son's old roommate, had also been thinking of my reading needs. She loves the tabloids. The hot gossip that summer was Princess Diana and Dodie Fayed. When I arrived, she had five magazines waiting for me, complete with total coverage about the new lovers, including the famous kiss. When are they going to get married? What impact would it have on the Royal Family? Everyone was speculating. This was the delicious gossip I was hungry for. Since I had been living in a world without newspapers, televisions, radios, or gossip magazines, all of this was news to me.

I felt good being with old friends, just talking, laughing, and drinking. They wanted to know about Germany. I wanted to know about their travels. Marcus had just graduated from Harvard Divinity School, and they were curious. What would he do? I had questions of my own. When would Scott, their son, marry Liz? The Martins had been on a long trip. Marlene's mother, Sheila, was traveling with them. Her companion was a tiny man named Alex who turned mean when he drank too much, which was often. It would be Sheila's last trip to Europe, and we all wanted to make it special for her. Marlene's husband, Don; her sister, Gail; and her husband, Braum, were the others on the trip. Sheila and I shared a bathroom and got to be good pals.

Sheila had been widowed for nearly 20 years. In spite of three sons, two daughters, and a slew of grandchildren to look after her, Sheila knew how to speak up for herself. In many ways she was more of a feminist than her daughters. I adored her. Sheila and my mother were born and died at the same time.

Before Portugal, my Aussie friends had been traveling in Morocco, driving a rented van. They would continue to Spain after our ten days together, then to Charleston, South Carolina; Los Angeles, California; and then back to Melbourne.

The next week we drove around taking day trips. We first visited Obidos, the city that was protected by a Roman brick wall, which allowed us to look out at the beach. It was a little cool to sit on the beach, which is what my friends would've preferred. We imagined what life looked like hundreds of years ago, and we were hungry to catch up on our lives. We also traveled to Carvoeiro, Algarve, Lagos, and Estoril. I'd never seen such a bright and brilliant blue as that part of the Atlantic Ocean. Although poor, probably because of a dictatorship, Portugal is one of the most marvelous countries

I had ever visited. Tiles made everything more magnificent; in Portugal, the churches, buildings, and even the road signs were tiled with blue, white, and yellow.

Though we traveled quite a bit, mostly we shopped, drank gin and tonics, and laughed. We spent our evenings eating delicious seafood from the area, whether eating in or out. The villa was antiquated; there was no television, but none was needed. There was so much catching up to do. We hadn't seen each other since I had visited them in Australia two years prior in 1995. Being in Portugal with old friends was my idea of a perfect holiday. I felt loved, wanted, and needed, but mostly, I felt like myself.

The telephone system at the villa was outdated. To make a long distance call, one had to call the operator and wait until the operator called back. Sounds simple enough, but the problem was that you never knew when the operator was going to call back. This was a real problem since all of our calls would be to Australia or the States. One morning around 2:00 a.m. the telephone rang persistently until we all got up, rubbing our eyes and wanting to know who had made a phone call. It turned out that the operator had the wrong number. We laughed until we cried. By that time, we weren't sleepy anymore. Marlene and Gail cooked breakfast, and the men made Bloody Marys. About 4:00 a.m., we went back to bed and got up around noon for shopping.

The telephone system in Germany wasn't much better. I was surprised that a country so superb in engineering, with some of the best cars and train systems in the world, couldn't do a better job with its expensive telephone system. I signed up for a service called *KallBack,* which allowed me to call home for twenty-nine cents a minute. Today, I pay three cents a minute to call to Germany from the States and four to Australia. The *KallBack* worked much like the system in Portugal, but you didn't have to wait. I would call a special number that was in Seattle, Washington, and they would make the call. There was a catch: after the telephone call ended, I was supposed to call to disconnect, which I often forgot to do, resulting in paying more for the time I used.

My Aussie friends always have to get their big blonde hair washed and set when they traveled. They could always find salons that would accommodate them. I couldn't imagine being able to find a place to braid or twist my hair anywhere in the world. After they returned from their trip to the beauty parlor, Marlene dyed my roots with an old toothbrush, like she had done many times over the years. After rinsing the dye out, I relaxed in the hammock in the backyard, soaking my hair with conditioner.

Gail and Marlene woke me from my hammock nap, equipped with a complete nail kit and new colors of nail polish. They pulled up iron green chairs.

"Don's snoring is driving me crazy," Marlene said.

"I want to slap Alex. I don't believe the way he speaks to Sheila," I said.

"He's a nasty little chap. I have to agree with you," Gail said.

"Good on you, Ethel, for thinking of Mum," Marlene said.

"I've never ever seen him this way before," Gail said.

"Maybe being around all of us makes him crazy," Marlene said.

"He's a little Nazi, if you ask me," I said.

"Ethel, you're living in Germany. You think everyone is a Nazi," Marlene said. We laughed.

"I'll get cocktails," Marlene rose.

"Ethel, that coral color looks fantastic on you," Gail said.

"That's so true," Marlene said.

"We've been meaning to tell you, Ethel, that you can't wear a black swimsuit anymore," Gail said.

"What color should I wear?"

"Any color: yellow, blue, green, or red. Those are some examples."

"Here's to color. May we always have it in our lives," I toasted. We sipped our drinks and painted our nails in the stillness of the lazy afternoon sun. I dozed off again.

"I'm afraid I hear our names being called, sister dear," Gail said.

"What?" I jumped.

"We're wanted," Gail said. She and Marlene took the clothes from the line on their way into the house.

"Someone probably can't find his socks," I said. Gail and Marlene left me to enjoy the rest of my nap.

Aussies are big sport fans, especially the women. Marlene had been trying to call home to learn the scores of a footy game. After she and Gail left, I continued to sit in the backyard. Instead of reading, I watched the white clothes flop in the wind like ghosts. The big sky was threatening a storm. I should've been working on my German. Instead I was reading an article in a journal with the acronym BIG – Black in Germany.

Germans like to think of themselves as being open-minded, tolerant, and accepting. To some extent, they are. Their school system and media play a major role in the lives of Germans. News is always world news, not just the bad stuff about Black males that I was used to seeing and reading at home. I saw documentaries about other cultures on the regular stations. However, their open-minded theory means that no subject is off-limits or handled delicately. Since they do not acknowledge that 'racism' still exists, there are no clear-cut boundaries, and nothing is taboo. Among my colleagues at home, 'political correctness' is at least a consideration.

According to the article, race is not considered a sensitive subject in Germany. Actually, no subject is considered sensitive to Germans, according to my students. Somehow I saw that as a lack of respect. Insensitivity leaves no room for compassion and understanding. Instead, Germans use language like *Ausländerfeindlichkeit*, which is not against all foreigners but those who aren't white. And there's the word *Neger*, which is associated with being "naïve, stupid, lazy, lacking in responsibility, primitive, being a sex-addict, AIDS carriers and subservient." *Afro-Deutsche*, *Schwartze Deutsche*, and *Farbige* are the preferred language. I did learn about a movement to change the name of *Negerküse*, meaning Negro Kiss, a kind of chocolate candy. Germans decided what did, and did not, exist: racism didn't exist nor did homosexuality, according to some of my students. I read another article about an Afro German woman, whose had a German mother and a father from Ghana. "'Afro Germans' like me know better than anyone else the depth of racism that still exists in this country, decades after the repeal of Hitler's racial purity laws. We thought a colorblind society was within reach during 1970s and 80s, but then the Wall came down, so did the first wave of racial violence." Walking in someone else's *Birkenstocks* didn't seem to be a concept my new world embraced.

The wind picked up. I was getting cold swinging in the hammock, but I was enjoying the oncoming storm. Raw sewage is a familiar smell in Portugal. Even that didn't bother me. I was happy to be alone. It had been the only time I had to myself since arriving in Europe.

In Kiel, there were so many people around all the time. Once I found a peaceful stream that ran into a small lake. I would take my lunch from the *Mensa* and spend the hour just being. Sometimes a blue jay would join me, other times a squirrel. One day, a young man came. "We've found the same peace," he said with no accent.

"It's divine," I answered.

"You know the Janet Jackson song 'The Best Things in Life are Free'?"

"Yes." I didn't have the heart to tell him that it wasn't exactly a Janet Jackson song. I never went back to the spot; it had been ruined.

The brewing storm was closer. The big blue sky was graying like the roots of my hair before Marlene dyed them. I enjoyed being involved in the drama of storm. First came thunder, then lightning, and finally the rain fell. I gave up my seat and went back inside.

I found Marlene crying. "Marlene, it couldn't be that bad, it's only a footy game," I said.

"Yes, it is." Then I saw that everyone had solemn looks on their faces.

"Did something happen to Scott or Leigh?"

"No," Gail said.

"But it's so sad." Marlene blew her nose.

"What is it?"

"Diana and Dodie are dead," Marlene said.

"What happened?"

My next memory was jumping into the van with Don driving too fast in search of a television or English-speaking newspapers. We dashed in and out of cafes and other places we had shopped. Everyone was crying in disbelief. Finally, after a third stop, we found a television at a small hotel. The commentator was speaking in Portuguese.

"What is he saying, Ethel?" Marlene asked.

Somehow, with my limited German, I was supposed to translate Portuguese to German, then German to English. "I have no idea." Everyone was getting on each other's nerves. I didn't understand why we were doing this, being so involved. It was an awful tragedy that we could eventually watch and read about in its entirety. Yes, I was crying, but it wasn't as though we could do anything. I was also angry; I needed this holiday. Now it was turning into a mourning mass for Princess Diana.

Sheila was the first to speak out. "All of this is awful and sad, but it's awful and sad for Dodie's family too. The Fayeds lost their son. We shouldn't forget that." Just like that she had calmed us. After ordering gin and tonics, we watched the television as the pictures told the whole story. We all stood in shock. No translation was needed.

The last three days of our trip was spent talking about Diana and Dodie. My Aussie friends spoke reverently about England and the Queen like some white southern Americans speak of Thomas Jefferson or Robert E. Lee. I wanted to get back home, to Germany.

As we flew over London the pilot spoke of mourning the death of Princess Diana. I felt like we were floating over sadness, a sadness that would be with us for a long time.

It wasn't until I got back to Germany that I learned that Mother Teresa had died too. Germans weren't making monuments of flowers to the late Princess or Mother Teresa. I felt broken-hearted. I hadn't counted on tragedies being a part of my pilgrimage. What was I going to do? What would Francis of Assisi have done? I wished I had been at home watching television in my living room, wearing old cotton pajamas and talking to my friends on the phone about Princess Diana and Mother Theresa. But I wasn't home. I was living in Europe on a spiritual and intellectual journey, and like a good German, I would soldier on.

Chapter 4

IMAGINING THE OTHER

There are two ways of spreading light: to be the candle or the mirror that reflects it.

Edith Wharton

Silence was my constant companion in my new world, especially on Sunday mornings. It became my favorite sound, allowing me to touch a deeper part of me, my soul. I rarely traveled if I had to be away on Sunday mornings. My flat sat on a hill above a one-way street looking down on the town. I lived at *Mörikestrasse* 8, which I had to learn to pronounce correctly for taxis and such. It was a bit tricky for me, but I asked my German friends to pronounce it about a million times. To my ear, they all pronounced it differently. Luckily, I had the best teacher, Silvia. Sometimes I had to say it twice for taxis drivers, which I only took if I came home late at night. Other times I rode the bus or walked.

Hegelstrasse runs parallel to *Wilhelmstrasse* where my office was in the Bretch building. East of *Mörikestrasse* is *Goethestrasse*. I felt at home among greatness, although the greatness was in the form of male poets. I never saw any streets named for female poets. I don't remember any buildings named for women in Tübingen, either. Was that feminism too?

A tall, slim spruce tree bowed outside of my bedroom window. I needed angels in the night, and the spruce tree became that for me: my watchful eye, my angel tree. Sleep came hard in my new world, and on the odd occasions when I did sleep, I felt exhausted when I awoke from long and extensive dreams. I listened to trees and birds on Sunday mornings. This was probably what Lionel Richie heard when he recorded "Easy Like Sunday Morning."

Since I lived on the first floor, rain was silent too. My Italian-styled, cream-colored, renovated house was used as an international house by the University. It could accommodate four families. Only one German man was living there when I first moved in; he was on leave from Canada. I never saw him, although I heard him sometimes and smelled his food, which always made me hungry. Later, a couple from Denmark moved in and, finally, a young man from Cologne.

Germans don't work around their houses on Sundays like I often do. It was considered a family day for *Wanderungerun*. One of Germany's many laws states an individual cannot mow lawns on Sundays, which I liked very much. I wish America had such a law.

When my son went away to boarding school in the 1980s, I started a new routine for my Sunday mornings: I indulged myself by reading *The Atlanta Journal Constitution* and *The New York Times* while drinking a pot of coffee and watching my favorite television show, *Sunday Morning*. Around noon I would go for a peaceful run, if it wasn't too hot. Afterwards, I'd take a long bubble bath and plan my week. Later, I'd go to the market to shop for the week, prepare my week's meals ahead of time, and then clean my house. Sometimes I would go to the movies with friends or out to dinner.

But in Morgantown, West Virginia, there was no delivery of *The New York Times*. I could read *The Dominion Post* in less than ten minutes. I couldn't run because the mountains were too hard on my knees and rarely were there sidewalks on the streets in my neighborhood near the campus. And most of my friends had their own families. There wasn't room to socialize for a single Black woman in that world.

In Tübingen my routine was as peaceful as the ease of the day. I got up late morning, brewed coffee, and listened to gospel music. I washed and dried my laundry in the basement. I was happy to have the time, since it took the washing cycle hours to complete. I was the only person in the building who used the dryer. While the laundry washed, I cleaned my flat and organized myself for the week, listening to the magnificent voice of Jessye Norman sing "Amazing Grace."

Afterwards, I'd spend two hours working on German. I devised a system by writing German words on note cards and taping them to whatever object it was. I felt like Miss Celie in *The Color Purple* when she was learning to read. Every night before I went to bed I would repeat the words out loud. Silvia was impressed.

Silvia and I had spent our last two meetings working on her proposal. I was pleased to be doing something for her. She had given me so much. We, American college professors, know how to write grant proposals in our sleep. Even though there is a textbook with 501 verbs, Germans rely heavily on only a few to carry their conversations. For example, the verb *habe* is such a verb. *Ich habe eine Pause, Ich mach,* which means, "I want to make a break." I felt good explaining to Silvia that verbs were the muscles of a sentence in English. You couldn't just say *habe* and *mach* for everything. Verbs help the reader to visualize the action. We wrote a strong proposal. Since Silvia had become such a generous and caring friend, I wanted to express my appreciation by searching for words, "grateful" or "appreciative." I found no German word to express my feelings. Saying *Dankbar* or *Spürbar* didn't sound like I was saying anything special.

At about two o'clock in the afternoon, all of my chores would be completed. Then, I would hike, which was one of my favorite activities, one I would never do alone at home. Germans value and respect their public space, since they have so little of it. Land doubled as the hiking trails ran through vineyards and gardens. The country is about the size of the state of Montana. Parks and streets were always clean and safe, and they were enjoyed. I often met families hiking after their huge Sunday meal. Sometimes I chatted with them, sometimes I didn't. When I did, they'd ask me to have a cup of coffee or a glass of wine. When I tried to speak German to them, they would speak English to me.

This used to happen in the *Stadt* until Silvia went to all of the merchants that we frequented and told them not to speak English to me. Germans were often looking for ways to practice their English.

After the outing, I would go back to my flat and soak in a long, hot bath while listening to Mahalia Jackson or Sam Cooke. In those golden moments, I was at peace with just being. I had never been given such gifts.

One Sunday afternoon when I arrived at my office, which was only a five or ten-minute walk down the hill from my flat, Bernd Engler stormed in.

"I've been calling you all day. Where were you?" He seemed annoyed.

"What do you mean, where was I?"

"I was getting worried. Have you met someone?" Bernd Engler asked.

"You know I am older than you are, don't you?" I walked in front of him and looked in his eyes.

"We're going to have to get you an answering machine."

"That would be nice." I put my book bag on my desk.

"Really, where were you?" Bernd Engler asked.

"I was hiking."

"With whom?"

"Not that it's any of your business, but I was alone."

"I see, but you need to be careful."

"Bernd, you're taking your host professor responsibility a little too seriously.

By that time, Horst Tonn walked in. "What's all the noise about?"

"I tried to call Ethel three times today and she wasn't home."

"Where were you?" Horst looked at me.

"Not again. Now if you'll excuse me I have to work." I waved them out of my office.

"One of the reasons I was calling you is that Lucy would like you to join us for dinner," Bernd Engler said.

"I'd love to see Lucy and the children. Thank you. I accept." I continued typing without looking up.

I didn't always go to the Englers for dinner. Sometimes I ate dinner at a restaurant with Horst Tonn. His family lived near Bochum, but he lived in Tübingen during the week and came back on Sundays. Sometimes I didn't go out but ate a light supper at home, thinking of what new German words I would need for the week. Even though those moments were challenging, I was determined to be a participant on this journey. In those moments of global grace, I found sweetness in my silence.

The month of February must be Black History Month all over the world by now. Flyers circulated around *Wilhelmstrasse* near my office advertising that Negro spirituals were going to be sung at the *Stiftskirche*. I thought the singers were actually going to be Black since the flyers showed painted Black faces. Lucy Engler told me she didn't think so.

"Why would they paint the faces then?" I asked. She didn't know, but she warned me not to get my hopes up. I wanted to go anyhow. Even if they weren't Black, I was still curious, and maybe they could actually sing.

I arrived at the church early and sat in the back just in case the singing wasn't good; I could ease out without being noticed. Not being noticed in Tübingen wasn't possible, but I pretended it was when I needed to. Sitting in silence overwhelmed me. Grandness and beauty ushered me into a silent prayer. How could it be that this church is so old? The church is known as *The Collegiate* because that is where the Universität originated. The keystones visible in the choir vault resemble those in the walls and windows of the Patron Saints of Church. It is dedicated to St. George, who was tortured on the wheel as one of his martyrdoms. The Patron Saint Mary is clear evidence that *Bebenhausen* belonged to the Cistercians. Count Eberhard procured new properties, thus the beginning of the University. My colleagues told me this.

When I first arrived in Tübingen in the late golden summer of 1997, I spent the first week with my new colleague, Harmut, and his wife, Ursula. Harmutt gave me a personal tour of the church, including to the top of the bell tower. Even though I was sick with a cold, it was a grand welcoming.

How many others had sat here with hopes and dreams? And sorrows? I felt moved with gratitude by the aura of such a space. I loved European churches. I grew up in a clapboard white church with a preacher who was called rather than trained. Here everything was so magnificent. Would I go to church if I had a church like this to attend? I prayed for all of those who would never see such a place. I prayed for peace on earth. Who could have dreamed that I, a nice 'colored' girl from Alabama, would be sitting so far from home? I wished that all the little Black girls would have dreams that would come true. I prayed that my grandmother, who had been dead for more than ten years, was looking down on me. I hoped my friend Alecia and her daughter, who had been killed on TWA Flight 800, had a safe crossing over. My emotions surprised me. I found comfort in the coldness of the church.

Programs and flyers had been placed on the pews. I waited like everyone else. And then it happened – the choir floated in from the side door. Lucy had been right. "Okay," I said to myself, listening to see if they could sing. They couldn't. Sitting near the door had been a good decision. I am tone deaf and don't know how to carry a tune, but I could sing better than the choir. Walking out, I didn't even feel guilty. I was too insulted.

I walked quickly in the brisk air to my office, laughing at myself. Lucy had been right; I knew it too. Germans don't see how blackface, like they used on their flyers, is racist. Maybe it wasn't on its face, but the problem for African Americans is that history often dictates our emotions. Horst Tonn was working. I went into his office and told him what had happened. He laughed.

"Are you laughing at me?"

"Of course, I am laughing at you."

We ate dinner and drank too much wine.

Afterwards, I walked up the hill to my flat and played "In the Upper Room" by Mahalia Jackson, thanking myself for having had the good sense to bring music on my journey.

My students liked *A Raisin in the Sun*: the acclaimed Pulitzer-prize winning play by Lorraine Hansberry, the first African American play to be produced on Broadway in 1959, with African American director, Lloyd Richards. The German library was much better equipped than the library at my University. They even subscribed to *Callaloo* and *African American Review*, the two most prominent African American journals. After we watched the film together in the classroom, I put it on loan at the library so that students could watch it again if they liked. Germans, even those who spoke good English, often had trouble keeping up with the language in American films, Silvia told me.

The librarian wanted to know if she could copy the film. I told her they could just have it since I owned another copy in the States. I was always trying to lighten my load of stuff that I would be lugging back home. Books and videos are heavy. Books, like so many other necessities, were more expensive than in the States. I would give most of my clothes to their version of the Goodwill, if any of them held up. Living in Germany was hard on clothes. At home, I wore all kinds of clothes and shoes since I was in and out of my car, but in Germany, they needed to be sturdy enough for walking, hiking, biking, and hopping on trains. My shoes needed to withstand walking in comfort and look a little stylish. I understood why Germans made such good-quality clothing; they needed them. I wished it had occurred to them to make some of those good-quality clothes in colors other than black, brown, or gray. In the States, clothes could be inexpensive if you shopped in the right places, and there are many right places to shop. Germans rave about shopping choices in America.

I've never had luck with university bookstores. In Germany, if the bookstore thought a book was too big or too expensive it simply wasn't ordered and the professor wouldn't even be informed. At least at home I would have been notified, but I struggled with that bookstore too. Before midterm, books would be sent back. Students complained, and so I called the bookstore and asked them not to send the books back because some students couldn't afford to buy all of the books at once. They always said okay but always sent the books back anyway.

German students talked excessively in class at the same time as I lectured. It drove me crazy. At home, I ran my classroom like the law. For a culture that believed in order, the talking surprised me. I couldn't hear myself think with all the talking. One day, I stopped class.

"*Entschuldigung Bitte*." I held my hands to the heavens. "We all may talk, just not at the same time." After that, they stopped talking, but they ate in class and made annoying noises with their food. I gave up. I was a guest and didn't want them to think I was unreasonable. The eating was less annoying than the talking.

More than half of the class was female, but the males did most of the speaking. I asked the class what they thought about the character of Walter Lee Younger from *A Raisin in the Sun*, specifically in two scenes: one, when he tells his wife that he's tied up with a group of people who can only grunt, moan, and have babies; and two, when he asks his family and the world, who's to say what man can buy his wife a string of pearls? Only the males answered, making excuses for the character, saying he was stressed out and wanted to change his life but didn't know how. They said the sister, Benita, was too bossy.

"Bossy or focused?" I asked. When no one answered, I continued, "What did the wife want? I would like to hear the females answer this question." I wanted their thoughts and ideas, not silence. The room stayed still for about three minutes. I felt comfortable letting the silence sail through the air. Females in the class not only outnumbered the males, but they were also smarter, or at least they wrote better papers. However, when it came to speaking up, it was the males who did, with answers not nearly as thoughtful and insightful as the female students. Feminism didn't appear to be a concept they embraced, at least not in practice. I often felt like I could have been teaching a class twenty years earlier.

"He was mean-spirited," said one female student.

"His wife wanted to be treated better, which didn't cost money. Walter Lee had bought into the materialism of the white man's world, in particular the white man he worked for. I wished his wife had gone upside his head with the frying pan," I said. The students laughed, which surprised me. I never knew when or if they were going to laugh at my comments.

"Maybe it had something to do with the way his mother treated him," a female student said.

"What do you mean? Her parenting skills?" I asked.

"Yes. The mother seemed much harder on Benita than she was on Walter Lee, or even the grandson, Travis," the student continued.

"Very good. There is a gender difference in the manner of parenting," I stated. "What does this have to do with you? Why is this literature? What are we doing looking into the world of the Younger family? Otherwise we wouldn't have a need to read and study it. Right?"

"African Americans coddle their sons more than their daughters," another student who had read some scholarship on *A Raisin in the Sun*.

"Is it African Americans or parents in general?" I asked, continuing, "How do Germans parent their children?"

"The same," a female stated.

"Let me guess, you have brothers."

"That's because of the War," a male said.

"Everyone has fought wars. How is yours different?" I asked the student.

"After the War, we lost so many young males. Now we show our appreciation to them. And we need to rebuild."

"I see, not like other nations. It takes more than males to rebuild. Females are needed to bear children. Right? But let's get back to the business of men and wars. Is that why my 42-year old, unmarried neighbor takes his dirty laundry home every weekend and return with clean laundry and enough meals to last for the week?" The students laughed again. Laughing twice in one class. Maybe they were getting me, or at least my sense of humor.

"Is that why the male students speak up in class more than the females, even though the females are generally better students?" I continued. No laughter. Silence.

"You see, *A Raisin in the Sun* is about all of our lives. That's what African American literature is. It's not just the lives of African Americans.

Someone from International Programs had fixed me up with an African American attorney who was working in Germany on some kind of military project. He telephoned me at my office. We agreed to meet at a nearby café in between classes. I had had enough of bad blind dates to know I wasn't interested in wasting too much of my time. He wanted to have lunch. I told him that it was a busy day, and I would be traveling for the next few weeks. I dressed up a bit more that day by wearing a red blouse and makeup, which meant lipstick. Heads turned when I walked to work, much more so than usual. I didn't understand until I got to my office and everyone commented on my blouse. It never occurred to me that wearing a red blouse would receive so much attention. I wondered how they would have reacted if I had worn a red dress. Then I learned that the silly woman who had fixed me up had told Tina, the secretary, and she told Bernd Engler. Sometimes I felt like she was his spy.

After class I went to the bathroom, washed my face with cold water, applied more lipstick, and walked to the café. He was younger than me, although I thought I looked better than he did. We introduced ourselves. He immediately gave me the story of his life, including how amazing he was, but mostly he wanted to talk about his interracial dating and how he loved to annoy the Germans. I sat stunned.

Instead of coffee or tea, I ordered a glass of Chianti. He spoke very little German so he kept snapping his fingers and speaking loudly to the waiter. I was thinking I'd rather be in my office grading papers. He continued to talk, and I continued to fantasize about where I would rather be. I would have rather been in German class than sitting there listening to this man talk at me. Finally, I looked at my watch and said I was going to be late for my next class if I didn't hurry. "But you just got here," he said.

I walked back to my office thinking I'd rather be in hell taking a German class than listen to that man.

Someone knocked at my door. "*Bitte*."

"How did it go?" Bernd Engler asked.

"How did what go?" I asked.

"Your blind date."

"It wasn't a date, but it sure was blind. Do you go around spying on me?"

"No, but I hear things."

"It was awful." I put my face down on my desk. "He never shut up. He thought he was something special." I raised my head and covered my face with both hands.

"What did you think about him?" Bernd Engler asked.

"I thought he was special too," I said.

"You know we're too old for blind dates," Bernd Engler said.

"Easy for you to say. You're married to wonderful Lucy."

"If I were single, I think I would just ask the person to submit a nude picture and write on the back how much money she had."

"And what kind of relationship she had with their mother," I added, then asked, "Why do they have to be nude?"

"To see what they have."

"Or don't have," I laughed.

Lucy Engler is a stunning woman with one blue and one green eye. She's one of the best cooks in Germany. She invited me to speak at the *Volkschule* where she taught adult education. My talk would be part of a program to help prepare German teachers to supervise high school students visiting the States for the first time. This particular trip would be to Charleston, South Carolina; Atlanta, Georgia; and New Orleans, Louisiana. Lucy wanted me to talk about the culture of the South and how it differed from the rest of the country. Of course, they had read Alice Walker's short story, "Everyday Use." So I suggested that I talk about Alice Walker and Flannery O'Connor, since O'Connor had been an influence on Walker's writing. She said they didn't understand Flannery O'Connor and, therefore, had no interest in her. Germans were always clear about what they thought and what they wanted. I like elements of clarity, but sometimes it left little room to explore and, therefore, grow.

My audience was very nice and excited to meet a "native," as they referred to me. After my talk, they wanted to ask other questions, like the difference between a college and a university. In Germany, there is no distinction: all higher education institutions are universities. They also wanted to know the difference between B.A. and B.S. degrees, since everyone who graduated from a German university earned a master's degree. The group showed more interest in shopping than anything else. I told them about places like Marshall's and TJ Maxx's, two of my favorites, and about outlet malls. This thrilled them more than anything else.

Their list of cultural differences between Americans and Germans were: 1. Everyone drives cars in America. No one walks, and when they exercise, they even drive to the gym; 2. There is something called raiding the refrigerator. Americans owned huge refrigerators, filled with foods of all sorts. Everyone was welcome to raid the refrigerator; 3. No one eats at the same time because of different schedules. In spite of all the food in the refrigerators, Americans still ate too much fast food; 4. Americans were overweight; 5. Children were often unsupervised; 6. Everyone drank water from the tap, if they drank it at all. There was no bottled water in all of America; 7. Americans watched television and talked on the telephone all the time, and, as a result, no one read books; 8. Americans were in too much debt; 9. Americans talked about God all the time; 10. Americans are more racist than other countries.

"This is an interesting list. Perhaps it represents some Americans. However, I would like to point out that America has a population more than three times the size of yours and more diversity than any place in the world. It would be impossible to categorize America," I pointed out.

"What did you say was the best place to shop for jeans?" asked one of the teachers.

I laughed to myself.

The next day in class I said to my students I needed someone to braid my hair. When I had first received my Fulbright fellowship, one of my colleagues told me I would never find anyone to braid my hair. I didn't think she knew what she was talking about since there was an American army base in Stuttgart and there would be African Americans there. Plus, I wanted to tell my colleague that I would've shaved my head if necessary to live and teach in Germany for a year.

This was the same colleague, along with her best friend, who had refused to leave my house after a reception for a candidate. My second year at WVU, I served on a search committee for a poet. Not only was the reception held at my house, but I also was responsible for taking the candidate to dinner to be joined by other members of the committee. The two colleagues said they weren't ready to leave since it was the first time they had been in a Black person's house. I told them to make sure the cat was in and to lock the front door when they left. I jokingly told them if they went through my things to please leave them the way they found them.

The Harlem Renaissance writers were eluding my students. At least Nella Larsen's writing was. She is known as the 'queen of concealment,' which is what 'passing' is all about. Trying to get my students to understand how natural it was at the time to conceal real issues under the guise of traditional venues, like marriage and children, proved more difficult than I thought it should've been. Imagination was proving to be more of a challenge to teach than I imagined.

We watched a film, *Against the Odd: Artists of the Harlem Renaissance*, which is about the Harmon Foundation, considered to be the financial machine behind The Harlem Renaissance. Artists have always needed supporters and will continue to do so. The film helped my students to visualize the glamour of such characters as Helga Crane, Clare Kendry, and Irene Redfield from Nella Larsen's novels *Quicksand* and *Passing*. It also demonstrated how class and color clashed. However, this didn't prepare my students to talk about homosexuality. Students everywhere I've taught are uncomfortable around issues of sexual orientation, especially the males. One even said to me that Germany didn't have any gay men. I didn't see any point in arguing.

At home, it was usually the few African American students who vocalized their opposition toward sexual orientation, usually via teaching evaluations. Once a student wrote that I should go to jail for teaching James Baldwin's novel *Giovanni's Room*.

In Germany, no one cared what students thought about professors. It was nice if they liked you, but student evaluations carried no power, even if they were given. After all, who was going to read them? At home, I found that student evaluations were more about popularity or how comfortable the students felt. Since I pushed them to challenge their preconceived notions, this was often not me. In Germany, there was no need for me to be concerned about what students thought about my pedagogical skills other than my own satisfaction of doing my job well. I believe most professors want to be effective. Student's opinions shouldn't carry such weight on a person's career. They often don't understand what good teaching is. But in class that day, my students weren't buying the scholarship of Professors Debbie McDowell or Cheryl Wall's argument that an envelope represented a vagina in Larsen's novel *Passing*. Students were a bit more convinced about Jessie Fauset's naming of sweets as a representation for sex in her novel *Plum Bun*. Only after hearing "I Want a Little Sugar in My Bowl" by Nina Simone did they gain an understanding of the point I was trying to make about metaphors.

Toni Morrison's, *Jazz*, is a great text to include in Harlem Renaissance courses. Her characters are ordinary and working class, reminding most African Americans of what their parents or grandparents' early lives would have been like. However, as the novel unfolds, the main character changes from normal to crazy, according to my students, who showed no empathy for the character Violet aka Violent. To me, she was a middle-aged menopausal woman, trying to hold on to what she knew and those whom she loved.

German students weren't obsessed with grades like students at home. They wrote only one paper per term but spent a great deal of time and effort on the work. I found their papers joyful to read. During my second semester, one student wrote a paper on the use of ginger in Gloria Naylor's novel *Mama Day*. I learned so much from that paper; it was deftly researched, written with passion, and a stunning form of art that is often overlooked. It is one of the few papers that I've ever read that will stay with me. That student completed her graduate work in the States and wrote her dissertation, which later became a book, on Gloria Naylor.

Bernd Engler had warned me that students often would not have their work completed by the end of the term. They were used to taking as much time as needed to complete their papers. He reminded me to announce every day that I would not be taking or receiving papers once I was back in the States. They must get them done by the end of the term. German students weren't used to such a strict rule, which surprised me again. I learned that they could receive credit from a course up to five years after they took a class, sometimes even longer, and if a student wanted to just audit my class, they could request a grade after writing a paper.

Three years after I lived in Germany, I received an email from a student who had decided to attend graduate school in Montreal, Canada. He would be stopping by Morgantown, West Virginia, to meet with me because he needed a grade for the class he had audited three years earlier. I obliged him. The only other person I made an exception for was a young woman who had a baby.

After class, I went to my office. Someone knocked on my door. The knock was too soft to be that of Bernd Engler or Horst Tonn.

"*Kommen Bitte*," I called from my desk.

"Professor Smith, I don't mean to bother you," said a nice female student with long dark blonde hair and serious brown eyes. She was a student from the class I had just finished teaching. Her heavy book bag weighed down her petite body frame.

"You aren't bothering me. Please sit down." I pointed to a chair.

"I want to thank you for what you said in class."

"You're welcome. Now what exactly are you talking about? I say a lot in class."

"You see, I am Turkish."

"I see." I nodded for the student to continue.

"I don't think they know since I look German, but you were so right. We are often treated, well, not well by the Germans. I think they hate us. Well, not all of them, but too many of them do. My grandparents came here to work. I am one of the only ones in my family to be able come to the University." The student pushed back her long brown hair that was falling in her face.

"Do your classmates know you're Turkish?" I asked.

"No, well I don't think so. My last name sounds German, and I speak the language better than most of them because I had to learn it."

"I see." I nodded.

"So, I got to thinking after reading the text on 'passing,' that I was probably doing the same thing."

"Well, there are all kinds of reasons why people pass. In fact, we all do it on some level. Remember in the Jesse Fauset novel *Plum Bun*, the mother passed out of convenience. She didn't otherwise value skin color, which is a different kind of passing than in Larsen's novels."

"I am very proud to be Turkish. It's just so difficult."

"Of course you are. Think about it differently; being difficult can be a gift."

"Is that how you think of being an African American?" The student asked.

"On good days." I laughed.

"My heritage is important to me."

"I wouldn't worry about it if I were you. What's important is that you know who you are."

"Thank you. We are glad you're here."

"I am glad to be here. I can also suggest some more literature for you to read. Of course, 'passing' today is pretty specific toward sexual orientation," I said.

"Thank you, Professor Smith."

"Thank you. You're really a good student."

In spite of walking everywhere and going to aerobics with Lucy Engler every Saturday morning, I still found myself gaining weight. It probably had a lot to do with the yogurt, which is the most delicious combination of pure cream and sugar in flavors of pear, kiwi, and coconut, different from ours. At least where I come from, they don't use those flavors in the same way. Plum is another fruit that is eaten and used widely in Germany. Ursula, Harmut's wife, makes the most divine plum tart. If Germans used a sugar substitute, I wouldn't have had to struggle with the wasted sugar calories that had snuck up on me. I needed to exercise more. And, of course, I was in Europe where eating and drinking were a way of life.

I've never liked aerobics, but that's what I did in Germany. I walked one mile to the gym and one mile back, hoping this would equal two days of exercise. Although Lucy and I had a good time after aerobics class, drinking coffee and making fun of the group, who had been together for years, I still wasn't losing weight. I wasn't even maintaining. It took me a while to learn the dance routine. The big-boned teacher looked at me and shook her head, "are you sure you're Black?" Everyone laughed. I did too.

I saw no sense in trying to tell her that I didn't have any kind of special rhythm like she had seen in the movies. Lucy explained to me that the teacher didn't want us to stop and rest during the exercise routine. I thought that was pretty ridiculous. One day, Lucy and I stopped. The teacher dashed to the back of the room screaming *"Faul, Faul, Faul,"* she yelled, pointing at us.

"She's calling us lazy, right?"

"Your German is improving," Lucy observed. After that, Lucy found a new teacher, a young woman from Argentina who was half Italian. We loved her and her music. She was so alive.

At home, I'd been playing tennis with the same group since I had moved to Morgantown in 1993. In Germany, I learned that there was no such thing as public tennis courts. You had to belong to a club. Bernd Engler told me that Dr. Weber, my more than retired officemate, was a member of a club and had been playing tennis with the same group for more than 40 years. A few members had died. I asked Dr. Weber about substituting for his group. He told me that he would check into it.

I watched very little tennis on television since tennis was only shown on television if a German was playing. Dr. Weber invited me to substitute for his group. My new tennis partners couldn't move well, but they could hit hard balls. They liked it that I knew how to work my way to the net, and put the ball away. I also thought they liked my short tennis skirts.

"*Schone*, Ethel," one said.

"*Zehrr Schone*," another said.

Germans never accepted each other's word if a shot was close to the line. This made the matches last a long time. Right before my eyes, they would argue about which one of them had undergone the most difficult surgery, taking off their clothes down to their underwear to show off their scars. Afterwards, they hugged, and the game continued. I took breaks by checking out the next court to see if there were younger men playing.

Later that evening, my telephone rang. If I had been at home, I would have thought something was wrong, but in Germany, a late call more than likely meant that someone from home had mixed up the time. "Hallo, Ethel. Here is Silvia. I am sorry to bother you so late."

"It's okay. Is anything wrong?"

"No. No. Life is good. I got the job. My proposal was the best one."

"That's wonderful, Silvia. Congratulations."

"But Ethel, there is a slight problem."

"What?"

"They want me for a semester, but they don't know about the children."

"Take their offer. We'll work out the children later."

"Do you think we can?'

"Of course, they want you."

"Good night, Ethel."

"*Schlaf gut*, Silvia."

That weekend Silvia, Klaus, and I went out to celebrate Silvia's success by seeing a film called *Comedian Harmonists*, which had won the Berlin film festival prize. Set against the backdrop of 1930s Nazi Germany, the film is less about the encroaching world war than it is about the music that defined the members of the close harmony-singing group. The Harmonists begin to feel the weight of politics as some of their Jewish-oriented songs come under criticism. Then their sheltered world explodes altogether.

I sat in the theater stone-faced, forgetting that Silvia and Klaus were with me. For the first time, I had some idea what Germans had lost. Hitler had cost them heart and soul — their art. The loss was so great they could never get it back; it didn't matter how many Audis or Mercedes Benzes they produced, or rapid train systems they built. The art was gone like the wind. The core of their being would never be again. No wonder Germans seemed so tortured, especially the men. Their loss had cut too deep. I had never heard music more beautiful, and yet so sad, than the soundtrack of Comedian Harmonists. In the States, the film is called *The Harmonists*. I have seen it three times since I left Germany.

I learned later that one of the members of the group was related to Ursula, who makes delicious plum tarts. When Silvia, Klaus, and I left the cinema we went for coffee to talk about the film.

"Wow," was all that I was able to say.

"Wow is right," Klaus said.

Silvia, Klaus and I are products of the 1960 and 1970s. Even though I had graduated from college in 1974, it had been the 1960s that had made my success possible.

"Do your parents talk about the War?" I asked.

"No, not at all Ethel. There is a silence in this country among our parents' generation," Klaus said.

"But I thought Germans loved to debate," I said.

"Not our parents. Not that generation. And not about the War." Klaus looked up. When he traveled in the States, he was often asked if he were an artist since he's dark with long hair and a beard.

"There is a belief that if you don't talk about something, it didn't happen, and pretty soon it will become part of one's memory, and no one will know if it actually happened or not," Silvia said.

"When there is no memory, there is no existence," Klaus said.

"Silence is very much a part of the tradition of slavery too. Total denial," I said.

"How was The Civil Rights Movement handled in your house, Ethel?" Silvia asked.

"It wasn't. I read magazines when I could. I had one history teacher who talked about justice and equality all the time. When he was fired, I was devastated."

"What happened to him?" Klaus asked.

"I don't know. I don't even know anyone who would know. I think about him sometimes," I said.

"At least you had one person," Klaus said.

"If I was watching Dr. King on television, my mother or grandmother would turn the television off and ask me, wasn't there some work I should be doing. I wanted to tell them that I was engaged in very important work, keeping up with what was happening in the world, but that would have been disrespectful."

"Did you feel scared, Ethel?" Silvia asked.

"I am always scared."

"Even now?" Silvia asked.

"Sure."

"What are you afraid of?" Klaus asked.

"Walking in parks, driving at night, going into a store to try on clothes, everyday kinds of things. Swimming pools, public parks, you name it. When something has scared you all of your life, you don't become less afraid because there is a new law."

"That makes perfect sense," Silvia said.

"Even libraries terrify me. And you have to remember, the murder of Emmett Till and the four little girls who were killed in the bombing of the 16th Street Baptist Church in Birmingham are the cornerstones of my growing up years."

"That's a lot. I would be scared too," Silvia said.

"And all of those assassinations." I shook my head.

"What else?" Klaus asked.

"That's not enough?" I laughed.

"Of course," Klaus said.

"I often feel cheated," I said.

"How's that Ethel?" Klaus asked

"When I hear my white friends talk about going to beaches for holidays, knowing how to swim, or playing in the woods, all without fear. In fact, they feel so entitled to have had such a childhood, which is how they should feel. My childhood should've not been rooted in fear."

"Is that why you don't swim?" Silvia asked.

"I took swimming lessons when I was and adult. I can save myself, but swimming wasn't a common part of my growing up. I wasn't allowed in public pools growing up, so I never had a place to learn. I would've loved to roam the woods, to be among nature. Instead, I learned to fear nature rather than appreciate it. Too many African American children were found lynched in the woods. That's one of the reasons I like hiking here. I don't feel afraid."

"What about in cities in the States?" Klaus asked.

"Less so."

"What else?" Klaus asked.

"Your turn," I said, turning to Silvia.

"What happened in Germany affected all of us. And you're right seeing that film reminds me too how much we lost," Silvia said.

"And we can never get it back," Klaus said.

By that time we were the only people left in the café. We traded our coffee for wine. There we sat from different worlds, but we were sharing a similar pain, the pain of history.

Chapter 5

MARCHING INTO THE NEW MILLENNIUM

in my dreams of roads

each turn glitters,

the road remembers your

footsteps.

each night is a crossroad.

and I must choose

a Babylon burning and be cursed

or reason.

mother, this choosing is hard –

Opal Moore

My first semester was drawing to an end. Teaching was great. Living in a country where I didn't speak the language made me feel like I couldn't do a lot. Finally, in my new world there was something I could do well: dress up. While Germans dully dressed themselves in black, grey, and brown, I liked getting dressed up with over-the-knee skirts, colorful scarves, and mostly white blouses. I wore my hair pulled back from my face with earrings, and a big-faced, Timex watch. At home, I don't carry a book bag because it hurts my back, but in Germany, it was a must. I read some-where that Germans have a high rate of bad backs; I think it has something to do with carrying book bags that are too heavy. The semester had gone by smoothly once the crazy American woman left my class. I was looking forward to the holiday season, when Marcus would come to visit me. It was the longest we had gone without seeing each other.

Students gave me the names and telephone numbers of three African women who could braid my hair. All were within a 20-30 minute bus ride, which amazed me. At home, I had to travel to Pittsburgh, Pennsylvania; Washington, DC; and sometimes New York City, to get my hair braided. The good thing about braiding was that I only had to have it done a few times a year, but it was still a drag most of the time. I was blown away to learn that hair braiding in Ger-many was minutes away. Other than my weekend hikes and travels to other cities, I had not ventured outside of the *Stadt*. I called Helen, who had been recommended to me by Tina Bach, because she was a distant relative of Tina's.

I felt like I had won a prize when I smiled into the warm face of Helen from Eritrea. She was training to be a nurse, which demanded a solid understanding of the German language. I was impressed. She and her family had lived in Tübingen for seven years in an area that Americans would deem the projects. I got a first-hand glimpse of what life looked like for a person of color, battling with a difficult language, and no Council on International Commission for support. My life was a fantasy compared to hers; it was not that hers was bad, but it was a far distance from my privileged one. Her house was filled with music and laughter. Her two children could speak German and English since they had always been in the German school system. Her oldest son worked at some kind of plant. He slept during the day and worked at night. The younger child was around more often, so he translated for Helen and me when needed. I tried to speak German to her, but I was sure she didn't understand.

Helen's house felt like a letter from home. This was the first time I had seen walls painted a color other than white or light cream since I had left home. Bright reds, greens, and light blues reminded her of her country, since they were the colors of the flag. Even though they were poor by the standards of Germans I had encountered, her house and surroundings were clean and respected. I've always wondered why poor meant dirty. I grew up without resources, but our home and yard was always clean, as was everyone's in our community.

Helen cooked and fed everyone around her. Her pots were always filled with spicy stews. I ate, but I didn't want to ask too many questions about what I was eating; it didn't seem polite. Helen's movements were as precise as the rhythm of an orchestra. Her never-rushed walk was dignified and graceful, contrary to mine, which is always hurried. Bernd Engler often laughed at me about being in a hurry all the time. I wanted to tell him that it wasn't a natural part of my personality, but I was task-oriented out of necessity, starting with raising my son on my own. I never told him since it probably would have made him feel bad.

Other than spicy food, the scent of lavender graced Helen's house. I often flopped down on her roomy sofa and laughed out loud, my way of being thankful for having found her. The first time I did such an act was by accident. She laughed too. When she braided my hair, we only talked between breaks as she creamed her tired fingers. I sipped peppermint tea and felt grateful to be in her presence.

Sometimes she played a video about her country. Other times she showed some video about African Americans like *Shaft* or *The Temptations*, which was funny dubbed in German. I often gave her a book or some other token of my appreciation. No one had ever braided my hair with Helen's skill and care. I always felt good when I paid her twice as much as she charged since I was getting such a great deal.

The only thing I knew about Eritrea was that it had been invaded by Ethiopia. From Helen, I learned that the women fought side by side with the men for their country. She took to marching like Germans took to hiking. Eritrea is the northernmost province of Ethiopia, on the east coast of Africa, between Sudan and the Red Sea. Its coastal plain is the hottest place in Africa. Eritrea was an Italian colony before the British captured it in 1941 during World War II. In 1952, it became federated with Ethiopia. In the early 1960s, civil war broke out between Eritrean rebels who wanted independence from Ethiopia, which ended up as 30 years of fighting. I read this later in a guidebook.

On my second visit to Helen's, she wasn't home when I arrived. I told myself that she was coming. I sat on the steps as I waited, reading and enjoying the golden sun of Tübingen. I heard "Dancin' in the Streets" by Martha and the Vandellas from a neighbor's raised window. Even though it was winter, the weather was warm that day. The music felt like it was raining down from the heavens. I was having such a good time that I forgot I was waiting for Helen until she tapped me on the shoulder. Her shift had run late. I handed her a bag of apples, oranges, and chocolate. She peeped in the bag and said I must have known she was hungry.

If I lived in Germany, Helen would be part of my family. I needed the presence of her spirit; she was a gift from the universe. She reminded me not only of who I was, but who I could become. Before I left Germany, I visited Helen and her family, bringing used clothes, music, and food. She gave me love and history. During my last days in Germany, she and her family cooked a feast for me.

The following week, I traveled to Friedberg to meet Rose-marie Abendroth, who had arranged for me to speak at the Goethe Universität in Frankfurt. She had told the American Studies professors, mostly females, that I was a relative. The truth was just too complicated: she was the aunt of my son's English teacher's husband. In Atlanta, Marcus's English teacher and her husband had befriended us. By the time Marcus was in boarding school in Connecticut, they had moved to Cambridge, Massachusetts, and their house became a home away from home for my son. They had even attended his graduations from high school and college. I will always be indebted to the wonderful people who supported me as a parent, especially Rosemarie's niece and nephew, Julia and Jimmy. Being a single parent is lonely. I had to make some hard decisions, and I was never sure I was making the correct ones.

Rosemarie is also an African and African-American scholar. She studied at the University of Massachusetts, in Amherst, with Professor Rhonda Cobham-Sander and other noted scholars. Although she didn't receive a degree, she is well versed and interested in the culture of America, especially that of African Americans.

She had described herself as tall and blonde over the telephone. I told her I was African American and medium size. Later, she told me that she was happy to see that I was in good shape because the African-American women she had known were overweight. It limited their physical mobility, and she was very active.

Other than that rocky start, we got along well and had much in common: our scholarly interests, artistic pursuits, and rearing our children on our own. If I had been a morning person, my life would've been easier in Germany. Rosemarie, like all of the Germans I knew, insisted that I eat a breakfast of heavy breads with local jams and warm coffee. I missed drinking really hot coffee. That was a big part of the pleasure of a cup of coffee for me.

My flat came furnished with everything, including a coffee maker that sounded as though it was going to conk out any second. I never liked the coffee. Some of my German friends even drank instant coffee. If I lived in Germany permanently, I would have to have a better coffee pot, cable to watch CNN, a cable-radio to listen to NPR, and a small freezer. I couldn't be bothered with going to the market almost every day.

Rosemarie is an elementary school teacher and had to be at school early, but she often came home for lunch. On the day that I was to meet my host professors in Frankfurt, Rosemarie couldn't come home for lunch but had arranged for her long-term companion, Manfred, to pick me up and deliver me to the University. Later, I would take a train in the early evening and meet her. Her house was warm and cozy and gave me the best sleep I had experienced. I felt like a family member visiting a favorite relative.

At the Universität, a student showed me around the immediate city of Frankfurt, which was one of my favorite parts of traveling and lecturing. Frankfurt felt like any smaller American city, maybe Cleveland or Pittsburgh. Although the city refers to itself as Frankfurt am Main, it is certainly not Manhattan. The city is the transportation hub of Germany. The Main River and canal system connects the city with the North Sea.

Allied bombers leveled nearly half of Frankfurt during World War II, including the birthplace of Johann Wolfgang Goethe, the namesake of Frankfurt's *Universität*. The city was rebuilt after the War with the help of America aid, and Goethe's home was restored to a museum. Rosemarie and I spent an afternoon in the museum. The city changed Frankfurt Universität's name to Johann Wolfgang Goethe in 1932, according to the guidebook.

Rosemarie met the group of female professors and me for dinner at a Vietnamese restaurant. The professors never asked how Rosemarie and I were related, which would've been the first question asked at home. They said they could feel our connection. I knew we were going to be friends for a long time. For the remainder of my time in Germany, she called to check on me, like a good relative would.

Back in Tübingen and all over Germany, thousands of students were marching in the streets, protesting the rising cost of their college education. I agreed with the concept of protesting, but it was hard for me to have much empathy for the students. My son, Marcus, had graduated in 1993 from Wesleyan University in Connecticut. Just to be enrolled had cost more than $25,000 a year. With grants, scholarships, and student loans, we managed to get through, but he was weighed down in debt. I was earning less than $20,000 a year, teaching as an instructor at Virginia Tech, and that was a good job. German students stayed at the universities too long. Not everyone needed or wanted a master's degree. I did understand how it kept the unemployment rate down, but it was a privilege they could no longer afford, I thought. I didn't express my opinion, though, since no one asked me.

In the halls of the Brecht Building, named by the students for poet and playwright Bertolt Brecht, American Studies faculty, staff, and students were listening to their radios as more students took to the streets. I was surprised and delighted. I felt sure that W.E.B. Du Bois would have been, too, since he had talked about how obedient Germans were. During that short time in history, Germans were neither obedient nor orderly. Therefore, for those students, this was a serious act of defiance. I was impressed.

In class, I offered students an opportunity to talk about their issues, such as what brought about the protests, or continue with the scheduled texts. They overwhelmingly opted to continue with the texts. Some students asked to be excused to participate in the march. I approved. Students wanted to compare what they were doing to The Civil Rights Movement. I thought that was a little bit overreaching, but it was their march. I wanted to tell them that during The Civil Rights Movement, people were jailed, beaten, bombed, and lives were often lost. Instead of fear, bloodshed, jails, or death, the streets of Tübingen were energized. I didn't want to undermine their efforts, so I said little to them. The Civil Rights Movement is too close to my heart. At every café on every street corner, people were engaged in debate, and everyone knew what everyone else was talking about.

"Why aren't you marching?" one student wanted to know.

"I am a guest of your government and will conduct myself according to my contract. Anyway, this isn't my fight."

"I thought the struggle for justice meant everyone," the same male student countered.

"Hey, I have to know what I'm fighting for. When I offered you an opportunity to teach me more about your issues, you declined. And now you think I should march?"

"Would you march at home?" the student asked.

"I don't know. It depends on how strongly I felt about the issues," I answered.

The classroom was silent as students tried to think of a way to further their argument with me.

"And remember, I am supporting you. I wanted to talk about your issues, and I am allowing students time out of class. Those technical issues matter. What are your other professors doing?" I asked.

"Most don't even show up, because they assume we're not going to be in class."

"Then the question becomes, what do you do with the time?" I said. "How do you make it valuable? This is your time in history. Not mine. Not your professors'."

"But we don't have time for this," another student whined.

"What do you have time for? This is your time to be counted and make a difference, but what will you do? What will be your future narrative?" I was pleased to have students who wanted to live with the times and not roll over like their Rs, students who were willing to take a stand for change. Their motive was self-serving, but at least they were standing up. When I compared what they were doing to The Civil Rights Movement, I concluded that these students didn't know how easy they had it.

The angel tree outside of my bedroom window danced in the wind. I called on my angel to help a friend. Mrs. Carolina Warner of Connecticut had died from a stroke. I asked my angel tree to assist her as she made her transition to the other side. Marcus had been close to Mrs. Warner and was having a difficult time with her death. Mrs. W. & Captain W, as everyone called them, had been stand-in grandparents for Marcus in boarding school. They attended all of his soccer games, graduation activities, and welcomed him and his friends in their New England farmhouse, which was full of

Irish Setters. Mrs. W, a Smith College graduate, loved Shakespeare and *Gone With the Wind*. Most of all, she loved her granddaughters and gave them horseback riding lessons and beautiful dollhouses.

Mrs. W had marched for Planned Parenthood during her early days because she believed that a woman had a right to make decisions about her body. For me, she had marched for my son at soccer games, teas, and graduation. Once, at a soccer game, a parent from opposing side screamed that they should, "Get rid of the dirty Nigger," referring to my son. Mrs. W marched again, that time to the headmaster's office demanding an apology from the school and parent, whom she felt surely had to have roots in the Deep South. I asked my angel tree to march with Mrs. W on her last journey.

No one remembered when Germans had taken to the streets in such huge numbers. I think of the French and Italians as strikers, willing to protest at the drop of a Lira, but the Germans were supposed to take care of their citizens. There is no such thing as real poverty in Germany, my students said. I asked them what "real poverty" was, and they replied, "like in America, where there are too many poor people." What about when I traveled to Berlin, Hamburg, or Frankfurt? Old women sat outside cathedrals, and beggars with babies were present on the streets. All of those places together are nothing compared to New York City, San Francisco, or Chicago. My students were right, although I didn't tell them that.

Hardly anything else was in the news, just the thousands of students who were marching in the streets every day. Bernd

Engler and Horst Tonn said the marching would peak soon and lose momentum since a holiday was coming up before Christmas. Holidays were interesting in Tübingen. First, there were so many of them, and second, they wouldn't be the same holidays as in other villages or towns. I had thought of Germany as an old country. While living there, I learned that every region had had its own monarch. As a way of holding on to some of its history, they held onto many of the original holidays.

All that day in class I couldn't stop thinking of Mrs. Warner and how she hated poverty and injustice more than anyone I knew. The first time I had met her was when I drove Marcus and Scott Martin, our Aussie friend's son, to visit college campuses. That was a mistake. There should never be more teenagers than adults. Since they were under age, I drove; I wouldn't have trusted their driving anyway. We traveled from Atlanta, Georgia, to Concord, New Hampshire, stopping at colleges and universities in between.

When we arrived at the Warners', she ushered me to bed immediately in the green room, which became my room. At first I felt odd going to bed in the late afternoon, but I gave myself over to the most marvelous gift of safe sleep. I was too exhausted, even if I had wanted to protest.

"You need your rest," I remembered Mrs. W saying as she closed my door behind her. Later, I heard her tell someone on the telephone, "She'll never get over this. It was too much for her." I drifted into a peaceful sleep.

I fell in love with Mrs. W immediately. She had so many stories to tell about her school days at Smith College with

First Ladies Nancy Reagan and Barbara Bush. She and Captain W had also been good friends with Bobby and Ethel Kennedy. Her favorite story was her decision to date Captain Warner because he wasn't a Yale, Harvard, or even a Princeton man; instead, he was just a Navy Academy student at Annapolis. We laughed when she looked over at Captain W and said, "He's worth it, I guess." Captain gave her that special smile. When I learned of her death, I felt sad, lonely, and far away from home.

Rosemarie telephoned often during those early days of the student protests to make sure I was okay. We had long discussions about politics, about which she was well informed and passionate. I learned a lot of German from Rosemarie too. Not only did she know English, Italian, and French fluently, but she also understood how to teach since she had spent more than 30 years teaching.

Just as it had been saved during World War II, Tübingen was saved again from the student strikes. Our students joined students in Stuttgart, just 30 miles away, because they would receive more coverage with greater numbers. During World War II, Tübingen had been saved by its hospitals and medical facilities. Every war needed medical facilities; for this reason, bombs were never dropped on the medieval town. I never felt afraid, I assured everyone who called me or sent emails. There was no incident of violence during those days of protesting.

Bernd Engler and Horst Tonn had no immediate opinion about the protest, at least not in my presence. They kept repeating, "This was bound to happen." The streets of Tübingen were nearly empty. I missed all of the activity. I caught up on my work and talked to Rachel on the phone a lot.

When I was an undergraduate student at Alabama A&M University in Huntsville during the mid-1970s, most of the student body protested R.O.T.C. being a requirement, and we also wanted African American writers taught in the main curriculums of English and history. I agreed with both. Why was R.O.T.C. mandatory? Why didn't the administration care about the history and literature of Black Americans? I still have a hard time imagining how stupid it was for a Black college not to want to teach Black history and literature. Is that what hating ourselves was about? I marched. Sure, we won, but I was a senior and wasn't there when the changes were implemented.

The only other time I considered marching was in the late 1980s, when I lived in Atlanta, Georgia. Civil rights leader Hosea Williams led a march to Forsyth, Georgia, to protest the fact that no Blacks lived there. They had been run out more than a hundred years earlier. I don't remember the exact story, but of course, it was motivated by race. Oprah Winfrey had even taped a show there. Marcus and I ended up not going. Maybe the march was called off or too many people were already there, but I do remember it was a cause worth marching for.

In the meantime, I struggled through the students' comments about when it right to take a stand. The Germans seemed so privileged to me. Would they march for me? Probably not. Who would march for me? Who had marched for my rights? Was that the appropriate criteria to apply to justice and freedom? These were hard and honest questions for me as I struggled with who I was and who I wanted to become.

Everyone was talking about the New Millennium. It was only 1998. Marlene, my Aussie friend, was sure we wouldn't survive until the date with all of the hype. What would it mean to me? Other than a marking of time, what would this new era have to do with my life or the life of my son? I couldn't figure out the transition of the Millennium in Germany. Expectations were greater than what I was used to at home. I needed to ask Silvia or Rosemarie. With all of the hype, I was beginning to wonder if Marlene had been right. Could we even survive?

When I was in the third grade, my teacher, Mrs. Taylor, told our class that the future belonged to us. She promised that we would live to see the year 2000 if we took care of ourselves, but more importantly, we could make a difference and participate in this "new world." Mrs. Taylor had surgery to have a goiter removed that year while we were on Christmas holiday. She died. No one explained to us what went wrong. I was sad for a long time. I thought of her often during those days close to the Millennium. I never dreamed that I would be living in Germany, but Mrs. Taylor would not have been surprised. I knew my life would be changed after the experience of living elsewhere, but in what ways, I did not know.

I ate lunch with Silvia and Tina Bach at our favorite Greek restaurant. Everyone seemed to have extra time with the strike. Tina told us that Helen was concerned about her participating in the march.

"Of course she would be," I said.

"But her fear is uncalled for." Tina looked at her plate. Her square glasses dropped on her nose.

"What do you mean? There's always danger in marching," I said.

"I would be concerned if my sons didn't march. There will be no violence, Ethel. It's not the German way," Silvia said.

"It sure is the American way," I said.

"Part of Helen's fear is that she's not a full German citizen, but I am. My mother is German. I don't have to fear that I will be deported," Tina said.

"It's so hard for Helen," I said.

"I know, but she can't project her fears on me," Tina said.

"But Helen is a citizen?" I asked.

"Yes, but not a full citizen, which can only happen via blood or marriage," Tina answered.

"Does she know how you feel?" I asked.

"Maybe you can talk to her," Tina said to me.

"That's a good idea," Silvia said. "She trusts you, Ethel."

"And what should I say to her?" I asked.

"Tell her not to worry about me so much. I am a German," Tina said.

"That's what the German Jews said," I pointed out.

"And please, remind her that I am an adult," Tina continued.

"There's a difference between intellect and emotion," Silvia said.

Tina was beginning to sound like my son, knowing everything. I was happy when the food arrived.

I dug into my Gyro salad. "I'll go over and talk to Helen."

Bernd Engler and Horst Tonn had been right. The protesting petered out but left a silent strain hanging under our golden sun. Maybe the New Millennium would change the world. Classes continued with hardly any mention of the thousands of students marching in the streets of Germany. Days passed into the next holiday.

One morning, ten days before Christmas, I awoke to a light snow under a pearl gray sky. Winter had found Tübingen. Buildings looked like gingerbread houses sprinkled with powdered sugar. With all of the excitement about the students taking to the streets, Christmas had sneaked upon me. Had I been at home in the States, I would have invited my students over for the last day of class to trim a twelve-foot tree, but in Germany, I would have to find other ways to decorate since I couldn't be lugging a pine tree up the hill to my flat.

Marcus was coming to spend Christmas with me. I felt as excited as a child waiting for Santa Claus. I hadn't seen him since the past June. I was planning a dinner party for my friends and colleagues on one of the days after his arrival. I would ask Lucy Engler which day would be best. Marcus and I had plans to spend Christmas Eve with some American friends in Zürich, and we would be returning to Tübingen for Christmas Day.

Marcus had been whiny about my being away for a year. Friends telephoned, informing me that Marcus was going to miss me or that he was having a hard time with my leaving. Excuse me, I wanted to say, the same Marcus I have to call and beg home for Thanksgiving? Plus, he's 27 years old with a network of friends and extended family. When would grown children stop needing their parents so much? I had spent most of my life being a devoted parent. I owned a new freedom, and I believe freedom is useless unless you use it. Determined to use mine, I had been willing to move to West Virginia, where I knew virtually no one to begin this new career. However, I had been a little worried about Marcus after the death of Mrs. Warner. It hit him hard. Talking on the telephone was always strained, and often we'd end up fighting. It was time to see my son.

Both Rachel and I were hoping that our holidays would go smoothly. Her husband was coming to Berlin, and they'd visit his parents in Münster. Marcus and I would spend most of the time with the Englers. Hartmut and Ursula had also invited us for dinner. Silvia and Klaus were hosting a small dinner party for us. Their sons would be there and so would Tina Bach.

Lucy Engler and I had shopped for gifts for Marcus and Bernd. She chose a lovely sweater for Marcus based solely on seeing a photo of him. It was made in Germany, of course. I am not particularly good at buying gifts for men, but Lucy is good at everything she does. I was surprised at how busy we all became with Christmas.

I liked the German holiday season much more so than ours in the States. There wasn't so much commercialism. People wrote individual letters to old and new friends. There was gift giving but not on the same scale that I knew. I wasn't bombarded to buy junk I didn't need with money I didn't have.

In spite of not having a Christmas tree, my still flat looked festive, decorated with poinsettias. Christmas cards from friends were posted around the room. White and red carnations from the Greek flower ladies hung all over my flat. I missed my Christmas dishes. Instead, I spread out a tablecloth with red flowers and then set the table with my regular blue and white dishes, adding white napkins. Once again, my music had saved me. I own a large collection of Christmas music and had brought some of it with me. I still enjoyed something of the Christmas I knew from home.

When Marcus had asked me what I wanted from home, I told him I needed canned sweet potatoes, Pillsbury pie crusts, Martha White's cornbread mix, and Stove Top stuffing. I could get pretty much the other foods I needed at the market. Everyone was excited about my sweet potato pie. Most of the German women believed in purism with their cooking. I didn't have the time, interest, or skill to make a piecrust from scratch. Earlier, I had invited the faculty wives over for tea. I felt judged when they learned, by asking, if I had baked the pastries myself. My Christmas dinner party would be homemade, of a sort. When I had asked Lucy about yams, she suggested I mix carrots with white potatoes and no one would tell the difference. I didn't tell her that the idea made me want to throw up. Clearly she had never tasted yams. Given my southern upbringing, yams are as important to me as potatoes are to the Germans. I can't imagine living without them. My mother and grand-mother used to say, "yams, de one food dat connect us directly to de ancestors."

Marcus had attended the Pomfret School in Connecti-cut from age 15 until he graduated. When he came home for the holidays, he was always taller. That was one of the disadvantages of your child going away to school. I sent my boy away, and a tall young man returned. He had not just grown in inches; he was forming ideas of his own that had nothing to do with me. A part of me always wanted to scream, where is my little boy? The day I met him at the train station in Tübingen, I could have sworn he looked taller, even though, at age twenty-seven, he hadn't grown an inch in years. His flight had been fine, and he was happy to see me. Finally, my family was with me. In my bliss, I wondered if I could live in Germany if Marcus was with me.

After Marcus graduated from the Pomfret School, he attended Wesleyan University, graduating with a degree in English. Between undergraduate and graduate school, he taught at a private high school in New Jersey. Now that he had graduated from Harvard Divinity School, he was return-ing to the private school for a year until he figured out what he wanted to do. He was interested in the business of music. Teaching was out of the question, he told me, because he couldn't make enough money to support himself while liv-ing in the New York area.

I was pleased that Marcus had taught high school. He'd always said I didn't work very hard, even though I was always grading papers or preparing for classes at home. Now that we shared a teaching experience, he understood how difficult and demanding teaching could be.

The piecrusts arrived a little soggy, but they had survived. I immediately put them in the freezer. Marcus couldn't stop laughing at me.

"When I asked you what you wanted, I thought you were going to say lotion, toothpaste, or even books."

"Did you have any trouble with customs?" I asked.

"No. They only asked about my German name."

"What name is that"? I asked.

"Bernard, remember, Mother? My middle name."

"That's not particularly German. Remember George Bernard Shaw." Actually, the name Bernard had been my grandfather's name.

"I didn't argue with them," Marcus said.

"They are mean-looking. Were you scared?" I asked.

"No. I have an American passport and an American Express card."

"That doesn't always do the trick."

"What do you mean?"

"I am always afraid of the patrols."

"Have they ever said or done anything to you?"

"No, but if body language could kill, I'd be dead."

"Mom, you can take off your boxing gloves. Everyone is not out to get you."

"I don't think everyone is out to get me, but racism and sexism are real in my life."

"I know. But relax, you're in Europe."

"Marcus, I am relaxed." I looked up at him. "How do you feel?"

Marcus was exhausted. While he took a long bath and a longer nap, I planned my menu for the party. Afterwards, I wrote Christmas cards while listening to Mahalia Jackson sing "Silent Night." For the first time, I felt the holiday spirit of Christmas. My son was safe and sleeping in my flat. I wondered if Marcus was correct. His world was different from mine. Even though he had faced racism, the combination of sexism and racism was more difficult for me. Was it possible that only Black women could understand what I was talking about?

Marcus and I took the bus to Silvia and Klaus' for dinner. David and Jonas, their sons, and Tina Bach joined us. Klaus and Marcus hit it off immediately, bonded by the universal language of music. Silvia called them "Mr. Music Men." They were in charge of music for the evening, providing a brief history for each CD we heard. David and Jonas were also having fun with "Mr. Music Men."

Marcus made fun of me speaking German. He said I was trying to sound like Silvia. Of course I was trying to sound like Silvia; she was my German teacher. We were having a festive time with delicious food, music, friendship, and conversation.

The next day, Marcus and I walked around in the *Stadt*, shopping for my dinner party. I was going to cook a southern dinner if it killed me. Chicken was not as common in Germany as at home, so I decided to bake a pork roast with potatoes and carrots, which would feed a lot of people. In Germany, there were always more men at my dinner parties than at home, and they tended to eat more than women. It was an easy adjustment: just cook more food. I would bake cornbread from the mix Marcus brought, adding eggs and milk. Steamed string beans would give me something green, and the sweet potato pie was for dessert. I could bake up to four pies. If there were any left, I would give it to my guests to take home, assuming they liked it.

"Mom, everyone here looks like they've lost their best friend."

"What do you mean?" I asked.

"Look at these people!" Marcus said.

"They're just Germans." I had gotten used to their hangdog troubled look. I didn't question it.

"Why aren't they happy? It's a beautiful day in a beautiful place. And as far as I can see, there is no poverty."

"Marcus, you don't have to look happy to be happy."

"I know that, but look at these people. They look at the ground. No one is smiling."

"Smiling is a cultural construct that doesn't seem to be here. I always feel them staring at me, but not so much with you here."

I knew there was something different about walking the streets of Tübingen with Marcus: no glaring stares. Being alone gave them permission to gaze at me, and they weren't even friendly about it. Goddamn these Germans. Or was it goddamn men?

"When women are alone, they're more vulnerable," my son said.

"No kidding."

"I know you know that, but you're having trouble with the theory being transferred to your reality."

"Thank for that theoretical insight," I said, laughing at my son.

Marcus and I joined the Englers for dinner on December 22nd. I can't remember what we ate, but everyone cooked foods that had special meanings to their family history. The same can be said for gifts. I gave Marcus the sweater. He loved it, and Lucy loved it on him. I gave the Engler children, Dorothy and Toby, Harvard sweatshirts. A friend from Boston had sent them to me. I received gifts, too, from my friends and family. My sister sent me a pound cake baked from pure butter, sugar, and flour. The Germans, especially Horst Tonn, loved it; he said he had never tasted anything so sweet in all of his life.

While Lucy and I prepared the dinner table, I watched Marcus and Bernd walking outside through the window. Though there were only two years between Bernd and me, I felt much older, watching my son with him. He talked to Marcus like he was lecturing, and Marcus was listening like a good student. They loved discussing American literature. Bernd was impressed with the cast of professors Marcus had studied with at Harvard. Marcus was impressed with Bernd's knowledge and passion.

The next day, we attended church with the Englers since their children were participating in the Christmas program. Marcus and Bernd nodded asleep in church. I wished I could have, but the church was ice cold. Everyone kept on their coats, hats, and gloves. Germans are very energy conscious and don't believe in turning on the heat unnecessarily. One of the things that drove me crazy was coming home after midnight from a long day of lecturing, wanting a long hot bath, only to find that some committee had decided that the heat and hot water should be turned off after 10:00 p.m.

Marcus and I were happy to get back to my warm and cozy flat. In the small kitchen, my tall and handsome son and I prepared food for the dinner party. To my pleasant surprise, Marcus had become a good cook. It didn't take much skill to be a better cook than me, though. I knew how to prepare a few mainstay dishes, but since I had been in Germany, even those dishes were escaping me. I got measurements mixed up. I mainly relied on the Greek ladies at the market.

"Now that I've talked to Bernd, I don't think all Germans are so tortured," Marcus said.

"That's very open-minded of you."

"Of course," Marcus said.

"Okay, let's make a plan. I'll prepare the pot roast, and you peel the potatoes," I said as I rubbed the pot roast with herbs from the Greek ladies. "Can you get that roasting pan for me?"

"Sure," Marcus said. Standing over six feet, he barely had to reach.

"You know, I really like talking to Bernd," Marcus said, handing me the pan. "He's so smart, so serious."

"He has a sense of humor too," I said.

"Mom, you've been in Germany too long if you think they have a sense of humor."

"I laugh a lot here. You also met Silvia and Klaus. They're my friends, and they can be very funny."

"Mom, what you've done here is great. You've made a life for yourself, a good one. But Germans with a sense of humor? Come on."

"Thank you very much." I kissed my tall handsome son. "It's what we do. We're Smiths." I laughed.

"Remember when I was at Pomfret? When I'd call home complaining, and you'd say, 'We're Smiths, goddamnit.'"

"How can I forget?"

"You're a Smith, goddamnit." We repeated our mantra at the same time and laughed.

"What did that mean?" Marcus asked.

"Buckle up. Get your act together. Game on. Stop whining." I reminded him.

"Boarding school could be cold, but it wasn't all the time," Marcus said.

"Life can be cold, but it isn't all the time," I said.

"Like now, life is pretty wonderful," Marcus said. We laughed.

The dinner party was a hit. After tasting yams, Lucy agreed that white potatoes and carrots were no substitute. My eight guests couldn't believe that yams weren't a part of their culinary culture. Marcus and I talked about how yams had come to America via Africa. With a room full of professors, we turned our attention to yams in literature, especially from writers of the South, like Ernest Gaines and Alice Walker.

All of the talk about southern food made me hungry for foods from my childhood: turnips, collards, fried green tomatoes, okra, cornbread, and blackberry pies. My grandmother, who we called Big Mama, used to bake cakes for the holidays, especially at Christmas. My favorite was the luscious coconut cake. We weren't allowed in the kitchen until she had finished icing it. I told my colleagues and friends how Big Mama used to bake yams in the fireplace and serve them to us, hot with butter. At the end of the night, there were enough sweet potato pies left over for our friends to take some home, and they were very grateful.

They day before Christmas, we took the early train to Zürich to spend the day and night with Maria and Michael. I had met Maria at a writing conference in the Netherlands in 1996, and we had stayed connected. She was married to Michael, a German; they divided their time between Switzerland and America. She had been pregnant at the conference. That Christmas of 1997 was the first for their baby boy, only six months old. They lived on the Gold Coast side of Zürich. I hadn't spent that much time with Maria. Getting to know someone at a writing conference has very little to do with real life.

I took gifts of *Stollen*, a beautiful poster of Tübingen, and a German Christmas ornament for the baby. We got along well. Maria served a beautiful, delicious dinner of salmon with capers, new potatoes, and baby greens. It was a lovely time, but I was happy that we were only spending one night. Maria could be too much the drama queen. She complained about everything: how much laundry she had to do, how the baby wouldn't go to sleep. I wanted to tell her that was what having babies was about. She had hired a Portuguese woman, who worked for several women in the building complex, to work in her house. Maria accused the woman of stealing her jewelry, but when she told the other women in the complex, they didn't believe her. She said the women were just jealous of her.

On the train back to Tübingen, Marcus thought I had been too hard on Maria, but I had no patience for her theatrics. I didn't tell him the story about the Portuguese woman, nor did I tell him what really annoyed me about Maria. She was one more of those crazy and spoiled American women, and I had already encountered too many of them during my stay in Germany. Maria had called me one night to announce she wanted to fix me up with someone. I thought that was nice. When I asked about him, she told me he was her driver. I told her that the next time she wanted to fix me up with someone, she needed to ask herself if she would go out with the person. If the answer was, no, I probably didn't want to date the person either. There I was, a college professor, a Fulbright scholar, and she a *Haus Frau*, a housewife, yet she wanted to fix me up with her help.

Marcus was asleep when the border patrols came around. I nudged him. I didn't want any trouble with these folks. I handed my passport over first. I felt less afraid with my German work visa. He then reached for Marcus' passport. Instead of saying anything, the fat-gutted patrol stood over us, tapping his fat finger on the back of the seat. I continued to read. Marcus looked out of the window. It had begun to snow. If it hadn't been for the patrol, we would've felt like we were in a fairy tale.

"What business do you have in this country?" The patrol addressed neither one of us in particular, like he owned the country of Germany. Everyone's eyes were upon us.

"I have big business in this country. I am an invited guest by your government. And this is my son. He's spending the holidays with me. Do you have other questions?"

He returned our passports and moved to the next seat.

"Wow, Mom, you were right."

"I'm really not afraid of them," I said. Snow fell steady and hard. I looked to my right; the man in the seat clapped his hands toward me in silence. Marcus and I smiled.

We got back to Tübingen just in time for a lovely Christmas dinner with Hartmut and Ursula.

Marcus and I spent the 26th of December, Boxing Day, with the Englers. Boxing Day is celebrated in Australia, Britain, Canada, Europe, and New Zealand. The name has nothing to do with clearing the house of the boxes and wrapping paper the day after St. Nick arrived, as many have said. The holiday's roots can be traced to Britain, where Boxing Day is also known as St. Stephen's Day. On this day, giving cash or durable goods to those of the lower classes is a common practice. Gifts among equals were exchanged on or before Christmas Day, according to my guidebook.

Two days later, with Bernd Engler serving as an alarm clock, I put Marcus in a taxi to the *Bahnhof* so he could get his flight back to the States. I had never been able to actually see my son off. When he used to return to boarding school, I would put him in a taxi to the airport. After crying for what seemed like hours, I would go to the movies and try to lose myself. But on that golden day with a lazy sun, I walked around the quiet medieval town of Tübingen with gratitude and appreciation, as my son marched toward the New Millennium.

Chapter 6

LILACS

The hearts of a woman goes forth with the dawn,
As a lone bird, soft winging, so restlessly on,
Afar o'er life's turrets and vales does it roam
In the wake of those echoes the heart calls home.

— Georgia Douglas

An organization called German American Women's Club (GAWC) from Stuttgart invited me to speak to their group. The league was established to assist American military wives as they settle into German life. A Tübingen member named Hiltrud telephoned and asked if I would speak to her group about the writer Alice Walker. They had read *The Color Purple* and had even seen the film. I looked forward to spending time with them since Hiltrud had been so friendly on the telephone.

At the luncheon, the white American military wives ignored me by sitting together in a corner smoking. None of the Germans I knew smoked. I learned from Ulli and Hiltrud that the American women weren't particularly interested in the activities they worked hard to organize. Mostly they smoked, shopped, and counted the days until their three years were up so that they could go back to their suburban houses stateside. I did such an outstanding job helping the members to understand the writing of Alice Walker that GAWC adopted me and invited me to all of their activities. Whenever I could, I joined them. They taught me more about the place I was embracing.

Between GAWC and lecturing, I didn't have much time. My interests had shifted. I felt comfortable in my teaching, and my ever-improving German language skills gave me confidence; I was ready to explore the more personal me. I had found a new friend in Ulli, who looks like she just stepped off of the pages of a fashion magazine: thin with blonde, short-cropped hair and stunning blue eyes. Like Silvia, Ulli and I hit it off. Her laughter is music. When we talk on the telephone, even today, the first thing we do is giggle. Giggling with Ulli is high art.

I joined GAWC for an afternoon trip to the village of Haigerloch, located in the *Swabian* Alps. A river into sections divides the romantic village; one is on top of some rock outcropping, while the other is lower. Haigerloch is isolated from other towns, which has helped it keep much of its individuality. To the world, Haigerloch is known as the 'cradle of German nuclear research.' A group of German scientists tried to trigger a self-sustaining chain reaction by neutron bombardment of uranium. First located in Berlin, the scientists, led by physicist Werner Heisenberg, moved to Haigerloch, which was safer during the war. The testing was done in the *Atomkeller*, an old beer cellar, according to the guidebook.

As we walked throughout the village, our host told us more about the nuclear research. Equipment had been shipped from Berlin to Haigerloch at the end of 1944. The laboratory and nuclear reactor were assembled in the former beer cellar. The scientists discovered that the size of the reactor limited the neutron production and their goal of creating a nuclear chain reaction could not be accomplished. The Allies captured the scientists in April 1945 and took them back to England, where they remained until January 1946.

While imprisoned, they heard the news about the two atomic bombs dropped in Hiroshima and Nagasaki. Most of the scientists were so upset at the deaths and the destruction caused by the bombing that some contemplated suicide. Their experimentation was not intended for use in a bomb, but for research. The reactor was dismantled and sent to America to help with the successful testing of future atomic bombs. The Allies were ordered to destroy the Haigerloch laboratory, but a priest took the chief of the Armed Forces up to the church above the laboratory to show what else would be destroyed if bombs fell. The chief reconsidered, and the church was spared.

Another name for Haigerloch is *Der Flieder*, named for the abundance of lilacs that hold the village captivated every spring. "More lilacs bloom here than any place," I kept hearing.

For the first time, I thought of home. I missed my front porch with the little gray sky and the sweetness of my lilacs. My wind chimes sang out to me from the mountains of West Virginia. My neighborhood was what I liked most about Morgantown.

Woodburn is an old neighborhood with a spirit of caring. In spite of the limitation of living in Morgantown, my neighbors, the Crosses, the Basferds, the Nicholas, the Tanners, the Lewises, the Murphys, and so many others have taught me what a community is by just being themselves. I hadn't heard wind chimes in Germany, although I had seen some in a store window. I considered buying them but decided against it; there was probably some kind of permit that I would need. Surely, I thought, someone must be listening to the music of wind chimes in Germany.

When I saw the lilacs in Haigerloch, thoughts of home were swept from my mind. I couldn't stop saying, "Wow!" Big balls of purples danced across the village, drenching it in perfume. I was enthralled and mesmerized. No wonder everyone was talking about lilacs. They hung everywhere, casting their scent and showing off their beauty. Had Walt Whitman ever visited Haigerloch? Even the military wives were in a good mood. Maybe it was because their husbands were with them. Ulli said it had to do with the romance of the lilacs. Haigerloch enchanted me; I felt like I was in a dream.

Ulli introduced me to Michael, who accompanied her. When I first saw him, I assumed he was her young husband. I thought, "You go, girl!" My assumption was wrong. Michael was the physicist and presenter for the program. Right then and there, I fell in love with Albert Einstein. Michael was researching the life of Werner Heisenberg and finishing his Ph.D. at the Universität Stuttgart. His presentation was excellent; he spoke flawless English, although I didn't remember a word he had said since I was more interested in him. I noticed him watching me, too, but pretended I didn't. In Germany, flirting is alive and well. Or was it that I was in the company of men who expressed an interest in me?

After the scientific history program, we continued the tour up to the church, which had been built in the 1600s by the princely pair of Christoph and Katarina von Hollenzollern. The church in the lower part of the village could no longer be cared for; a new one needed to be built for the graves of the newly interred line of the Hohenzollern family.

One hundred and fifty years after it was built, Prince Joseph Friedrich von Hollerzollern declared the church Baroque, as he moved into the castle above. His heart is supposed to be in the crypt of the church. Maybe Ulli was right about the romance associated with Haigerloch. The high altar of the church is made of gold and silver, and the walls are covered with a riot of frescoes. I predicted romance and beauty in my future.

Walking further up, the church castle is a photogenic jumble of Renaissance buildings that dominate the skyline of the village. After the tour, Ulli and I walked around in the old Jewish cemetery that dated as far back as the 16th century. Jews had rented dwellings in the town until 1780, when the town ordered them to settle in its "Haag" district. Before the War, the Jewish quarter was home to more than 200 Jews, but during the War, all were deported to concentration camps. Only eleven people survived.

A synagogue was built at its center in 1783 but was destroyed in 1938. The building is now restored, along with the structure next door, which in former times had housed the *mikve*. A nearby building for the Jewish community center, erected in 1844, was also renovated; it contained classrooms and residences for the rabbi and schoolteachers. The old cemetery is in a forest near Weldorf. Only a few stones still exist, as it hasn't been in use since 1804.

An eerie kind of beauty is cast over the cemetery with its ivy-covered gravestones, worn from weather and age. Hebrew is written on the oldest headstones; Yiddish is written on the others. We saw very few new headstones. Haigerloch's Jewish cemetery is unusual since most Jewish cemeteries were outside of village boundaries. Michael followed Ulli and me, taking photos of us, me in particular.

"I think he has found his subject," Ulli giggled.

Michael is from Celle between Hannover and Hamburg. He said he was from up North, the greatest place on earth. His mentor was his only reason to be in *Swabian* land. Ulli told me that Michael's mentor was her husband's best friend. She also informed me that Michael was one of the most brilliant minds in physics. I was beginning to like all aspects of the handsome German, especially the way he walked, moving his hips like Richard Gere. He is tall with dark, curly hair that's almost salt 'n' pepper, clearly premature. His teeth aren't quiet straight, but when he smiles, it lights up his sea-blue eyes. He swept me off of my feet, and I allowed him to do so.

I had had a few dates other than the first self-absorbed man who talked at me, but they never got beyond the beginning. There had been a Steve, but he didn't have a chance after I met Michael. I was never interested in invest-ing in more than three dates with a new man, and that num-bered needed to be reduced to two, since I was leaving soon. Time was something I didn't have, and therefore, it grew more valuable. Learning not to waste time on mean-ingless men was a good skill, not just in Germany, but in life.

I had met another German man in the coffee shop I sometimes went to between classes to clear my head. After three dates, I told him I was learning German and didn't want to speak English. What I really meant was that I was going to try and not speak English. I had a knack of starting a sentence in German but getting stuck in mid-sentence and shifting back to English. On that fateful third date, I got stuck on the word *ungewöhnlich* in the middle of the sen-tence and reverted to English. My stern date told me that I was shallow and flaky like all Americans who couldn't say what they meant. That was the end of that.

I had also gone out a few times with my 42-year-old neighbor, who went home every weekend for clean laun-dry and enough food to last for the week until he returned once more. He rode horses, and I loved horses. We liked the horses more than each other. Yet he intrigued me, showing up in my dreams over and over as a monkey. Maybe some of my childhood memories got mixed up with him.

I never figured out the culture of dating German men. Maybe it had to do with the fact that I am not good at dat-ing in any culture. German men could actually be friends with you without wanting to sleep with you, or so I was told. You could also go out with them for a long time and nothing would happen, even if he did want to sleep with you. The slow pace drove me nuts in the beginning, but it had served me well not to be in such a hurry. It's part of my task-oriented approach.

Germans seem to believe that having sex is more natural and honest than many Americans do. I couldn't figure anything out about my neighbor, just that he loved horses and seemed to want to get to know me without getting close to me. We talked on the telephone for hours at a time. He lived less than 200 steps away, but most of our relationship took place via telephone, except the few times we went out to dinner and to the stables. I counted on the angel tree at my window to guide me. What else could I do? I liked him. The fact that he never entered my flat saved a lot of time, and he offered me companionship without complications.

For weeks, a tiny bald man waited for me outside of the *Mensa*, student center, which I had to walk through to get to and from my office. He was always guessing which African country I was from. I was never afraid; his manner and tone were friendly, and I was bigger than he was. He appeared one day with a bouquet of wild flowers, declaring that he had figured out where I was from, and he should have guessed before. "South Africa," he said, walking fast to keep up with me.

The next week I finally told him that I was an American. He told me that was good since he had always felt sorry for American Blacks. I told him I didn't need his pity.

Bernd Engler asked me if I wanted him to have a word with him.

"And what word would that be?" I asked.

"You should be more serious about these matters."

"Yeah. Right." Obviously, I wasn't interested in telling Bernd or Horst Tonn about my encounters with men.

After the tour, Ulli, Michael, and I sipped white wine. I was intrigued with Michael, and he was captivated with my braids. Thank you, Helen. I asked him if he wanted to touch them. He said yes, and he never stopped touching them or me. He asked me for a date for the next day, Sunday. I liked that Michael was interested and assertive. I was to meet him at the train station in Stuttgart at 10:00 a.m.

Ulli telephoned and told me that Michael had talked about me all the way to Stuttgart. She thought he was a good one, and he was even interested in coming to America. My head and heart were spinning to the tune of Aretha Franklin's "You Make Me Feel Like a Natural Woman." This had to be the real thing; it even felt so right, better than I'd felt in a long time about a man. Does that make it love? When do you know it is? Maybe there was no such thing as knowing for sure. I wished it had been the beginning of my year rather than the end. If it were the beginning, I wouldn't have to feel so rushed. Could love be so simple?

Ulli was going to ask her husband to inquire from Michael's mentor if there was anything we should know, like his pattern with women. Falling in love is supposed to happen when you were elsewhere, particularly a place as ancient and awe-inspiring as Tübingen. How could one not fall in love here? It inspired the kind of love that Shakespeare wrote about, but I had to consider his tragedies too.

Later that night, I telephoned Rachel. We compared notes about men, how you know if they are the real deal. Rachel's marriage was strained from living apart: she in Berlin and her husband in Boston. Traveling was also tiring; when they finally reunited, they were exhausted. Relationships are complicated, we decided during our long girlfriend talk. At the end of the conversation, she said, "Ethel, Michael is the luckiest man I know."

Sleep came easy and soft that night. Huge lilacs unfurled into flounces. I dreamed I was sleeping inside of the magnificent blossom, and lilacs were tugging at my heartstring.

I met Michael at the train station on an easy Sunday morning wearing black linen knee shorts and a white cotton sweater set, which was perfect for the late April weather. I had brought five of such sweater sets with me. I looked good, but not too good. I gave Michael a copy of James Baldwin's, *Another Country*. He had told me he always wanted to read it.

God, I wasn't dreaming. He's gorgeous! Tall and fine, smart and funny. Is he really a German? Most of the German men I knew had a bit of that tortured soul personality trait, which I found deadly. Michael is an only child. His mother is a retired dance teacher, and his father had been a conductor for the train system before he had retired. His father, uncle, and aunt were from the East, as they called it. They had left before World War II. The aunt lived near Princeton, New Jersey, and the uncle lived in South Africa. His South African cousins were the closest he had to siblings. He visited them once a year and was in love with South Africa. I think he was surprised when I didn't express too much interest in South Africa. I adore Nelson Mandela, but I am afraid of South Africa; there is too much pain for me. My reference in the world wasn't associated with the concept of loving a land. Growing up in rural Alabama, politics had choked any hope of love of land out of me. I didn't know how to explain that to him, so I said nothing.

We walked around in Stuttgart holding hands, happy as only new lovers could be. I liked it that Germans held hands; it says to the world, this is my lover. As the sun was preparing to set, he showed me the *Schloss Solitude*. Michael kissed me for the first time in front of the fountain of the *Staatsheater*. His kisses were as light as lilac petals. "I've wanted to do that since the first time I saw you," Michael said.

"I've wanted you to do that since the first time I saw you," I echoed.

He kissed me again.

"Why aren't you married or taken? Are you any one of those things?" I felt bold enough to ask. Looking into his sea blue eyes, I liked it that I felt good enough to get to the point. It's difficult trying to get to know someone. He wanted me to ask those questions and liked explaining himself.

"No. No, I am totally free. All of my friends say the same thing. I don't know. University has taken such a long time, but I think I could be ready now." Michael not only held my hands, but also kissed them often. I would have to get manicures.

"I see." Being totally free sounded like soul music to this sister's ears.

"Let's have a drink. I want to show you one of my favorite places."

We walked past the *Königbaun* to the most charming glassed café. All views were spectacular.

"How old are you, Ethel?" Michael asked almost before we could settle into our seats.

"Older than you." I smiled, trying to remember not to give away too much information about myself. I looked good. It's the number one mistake women make, Rachel and I had decided, and I didn't want to make any mistakes with this man.

"I'm 36," he volunteered.

"I'm 44 and have a grown son." Why had I said 44 instead of the truth, 46? It really isn't that much of an age gap, but I wanted to keep it in the single digits. Ten years seemed just too long. Maybe I had been reading too much Nella Larsen, the Harlem Renaissance writer. "I am too old to have babies." I had always wanted more children but had never been in a good situation to do so. Ulli had advised me to be honest about what was absolutely non-negotiable.

"What's your son's name?"

"Marcus. He lives in the New York City area." Only answer the question. Try and not give too much information, I reminded myself. Don't tell him that your son was a gradu-ate student until last year. Whatever you do, don't give any information that he can use to calculate your age – like what year you graduated high school or that you started graduate school at 37. Michael and I seemed like such a good match. We even had matching birthday signs, Aries. Since it was still April, we thought a celebration was in order.

I had spent my birthday in Venice with Donna Blagg, an American who had come to Tübingen as a student and stayed. That was more than 25 years ago. Donna is tall and striking, a red head with green eyes. She is a successful entrepreneur and a good resource for Americans who come to Germany. She teaches English and German to business people who need to expand their language skills. Her German is excellent, of course, and she likes to interact with Americans to learn what's happening in her home country. We hung out together and traveled on many holidays when our schedules allowed.

Michael's mother had been pleased that he wasn't born on Hitler's birthday, April 20th. Bernd Engler's parents must have also cheered when he was born on April 21st. I was told that Germans often go without sex during the month of July for fear of having a baby on Hitler's birthday. I am sure it would have been considered a curse.

"I would like to be a father, but that doesn't necessarily mean a biological one," Michael said.

"Marcus is too old for you to parent." I was hoping that would put an end to baby talk. It was too soon.

"No, I meant adoption. What do you think about that?" Michael asked.

"I don't know. I've never thought about it."

Michael reached in his pocket and gave me an envelope. "Read this tonight before you go to bed, and spend some time thinking about adoption."

I was so stunned; I couldn't react. What was happening to me? Had I found *the man* rather than a man? We ate dinner at the charming café in blissful silence. I have no memory about what we ate or what it tasted like. Every time I looked up, Michael's eyes were glued to me.

After dinner, Michael walked me to the train station and stayed until I was safely seated on the last train to Tübingen. I couldn't wait to open the envelope. As soon as the train pulled off, I eased the envelope from my purse and opened it to find a lovely handwritten letter from Michael, telling me that he valued every moment we had spent together and that our future was bright. I smiled. There were three short stories by Wolfgang Borchert, his favorite German writer: "Hamburg," "The Outside Man," and "Rats Do Sleep at Night." I read Michael's letter three times before I slipped it back into my purse. Was there anything wrong with this man, Michael? I was good at spotting trouble with men. I can usually figure them out after two dates, if not before. No one was that perfect. There has got to be something wrong. We never talked about race. Was that a key? Would that be a problem at home? Did I have to talk about race? Could I not talk about race?

On a misty Monday morning while walking in the *Stadt*, I told Silvia about Michael. She liked the way he sounded and thought we should have a party so everyone could meet him. In that way, it would keep Bernd Engler and Horst Tonn quiet. Silvia also reminded me, as she often did, that there were still good men in the world.

"Oh, Silvia, I still have so many trips to take: Berlin for a lecture and a visit with Rachel. There's still Graz, Austria, and Munich." I flopped down in a chair at the café.

"Maybe Michael would want to go with you." Silvia sipped her tea.

"I don't think so. He has so much work before finishing up his degree."

"Well, what you should do is plan a trip together, one that has nothing to do with work. You can learn a lot about a person if you travel with them, especially a man."

"That's a good idea." During our lunch, the glorious sun spilled through the large glass window.

Michael telephoned that night to tell me about his research, but mainly he wanted to say how much he hated being away from me. When could he see me? I said soon and told him about my traveling. He said that was okay, since he had already planned a ten-day trip to Pretoria, South Africa. He already had his ticket. That would give me time to finish up my work.

"Maybe we could go on a trip when we're finished," I said.

"That's a marvelous idea. Where would you like to go?"

"My friend Trish invited me to Prague. Not to work, but for a visit. I am sure she would love to meet you too. Then I was thinking we could go to Vienna."

"I would go anywhere with you. Plus, I've never been to either of those cities," Michael said.

"I'll work out the dates with Trish and get back to you."

"I was thinking that maybe we could spend this weekend together before all of the work starts."

"I'd like that very much."

"It's going to be hard not seeing you until then. Good night, darling."

I ate lunch with Hiltrud and Ulli the next day, a non-teaching day. Ulli was happy to report that Michael's mentor had said Michael is a serious young man, with a big heart and bigger dreams. You've got to like that. The mentor could not recall any particular pattern, good or bad, Michael had with women. The idea of patterns with men and women is an American culture difference, I assumed.

I felt like queen for a day. Falling in love was wonderful, but I still had questions since we hadn't known each other long. I was too old to make major mistakes of the heart. After all, living together was more difficult than being in love. Or was it? Was I being too practical? Did anyone ever know when it was right? I had always thought love would come when I was ready. What did that really mean? What was I afraid of? I had worked so hard raising my son and building a career. Finally, it all had paid off. What about this aspect of my life? Love is such fickle business, so hard to be sure.

"Now, you know we will take credit for this," Ulli said, tasting her white wine.

"Is all of this moving too fast?" I asked.

"Who knows? I met my husband, and we were married six months later." Hiltrud picked at her salad. Her red nails were freshly painted.

"Ethel, you have to remember, we see the way he looks at you. And how he talks about you," Ulli said. We toasted our glasses of wine to love and following our hearts.

Two days later, I traveled to gorgeous Graz, which was a challenging twelve hours by train. The Austrian patrols were as mean as the German and Swiss ones. I arrived late at night and was a little afraid. What would I do if Roberta, my host professor, wasn't waiting? I did have her telephone number. To my ears, Austrians spoke slower than the Germans, which made it easier for me to understand their German. Although most of my traveling had gone okay, it was still nerve-racking.

Roberta did meet me, and we went out for dinner. I had been so nervous that I had forgotten how hungry I was. Afterwards, she drove me to the charming *Pension Rückert* at Rückertgasse, which was run by a Swedish woman. By that time, it was after midnight; I was exhausted. All I wanted to do was crawl into bed. My packed schedule would begin at ten o'clock the next morning. Despite my fatigue, I still had to be introduced to the Swedish woman. I got out of her car and headed to the door.

"Ethel, I forgot, here's something for you." Roberta caught up with me.

"Thank you." I thought it was my schedule, but instead, it was a postcard from Michael, telling me to call him no matter how late it was so he would know that I had gotten there safely. He wrote of how he missed me. I knew this was love. I didn't have to be afraid anymore.

"Somebody's in love," Roberta said. We giggled like teen-aged girls. My host greeted us and showed me to my room.

I telephoned Michael. He said that he could sleep now, knowing that I had gotten there safely. He wanted to know all of the details of my trip, even what I had eaten for dinner. I told him everything, including how the Austrian German was easier for me to understand.

"*Schlafe Gut,*" I said.

"I would sleep better if you were here," Michael said.

"*Ich Auch.*"

Graz is the center of the Steiermark region in Austria. Though it is the second largest Austrian city, it is composed of smaller parts: villages that were once independent, like much of Germany. It wasn't until the 19th and 20th centuries that all of the smaller villages developed. One of the most beautiful features of the city is that it is located in a valley, surrounded by mountains. Everyone kept repeating the history to me, especially the students. I was impressed.

The Mur River flows through its center. Archaeologists have found artifacts from the early Stone Age to the Roman Era in the area known as Graz. The streets that surround the city center stretch out in all directions, connected by small alleys. Buildings fill up the web-like structure. Seventeen districts surround the city in a circular format; their contemporary social fabric reflects not only when they were built, but also the circumstances of their growth, as well as their economic importance. I read this on the train in a travel book.

My stay in Graz was five days, but it felt more like ten. I was having a good time, but I wanted to get back to Michael. I gave a lecture on "Black and Female Writers in the United States," which was well received. Giving lectures didn't bring the same satisfaction as it had earlier. I was tired, but mostly I was in love and wanted to be with my lover, so we could talk and plan our future.

Just like old married couples, Michael and I started finishing each other's sentences. I took it as a sign that we were right together, and he agreed. Michael showed no sign of the tortured soul personality I associated with German men, though he did spend too much time telling me how much of a feminist he was. I didn't want to be told who someone was; I wanted to be shown. That aspect was workable, though. Rosemarie had been right: younger men can be more manageable, especially if they were in love with you.

After my talk, I ate lunch with two students at the *Mensa*. They gave me a tour of the *Altstadt,* old town, which consists mainly of rows of half-timbered houses, many of which date back to Medieval Times. The *Schlossberg*, The City Park, and the Mur River separate the *Altstadt* from the rest of the city, recently named 'World Cultural Heritage.'

Afterwards, I gave an afternoon lecture on my book in progress. A wine and cheese reception was given in my honor. Our group dined together later.

The next day, I gave two talks at high schools, one on the poetry of Langston Hughes and Rita Dove. Many Germans were interested in Rita Dove. I wasn't a poet, but I often taught *Thomas and Beulah*, her Pulitzer Prize-winning narrative poetry book. Rita Dove was popular in part because she had been a Fulbright student at Tübingen twenty-five years before me, where she had met and married a German.

Roberta, my host professor, asked me if I needed anything. I told her I would like to go shopping and see the *Universität* bookstore. Unlike most university bookstores in the States, most German universities didn't carry souvenirs, such as tee shirts, mugs, stickers for cars, etc.

A lovely Austrian woman took me to some shops in the *Stadt* that specialized in Austrian-made goods. As we walked and shopped, she gave me bits and pieces of the history of her country. I bought handmade blue and white linen place mats. In spite of the mean border patrols and Hitler, I still had a warm spot in my heart for a place that has an official costume.

We drank espresso at an outdoor café in the warm spring sun. She talked about the importance of femininity, women wearing beautiful dresses, which is part of local tradition. Young people weren't interested in the tradition; they were more interested in dressing like what they see on television. She also talked about the high suicide rate in Austria. Many males killed themselves because of the pressure to ski. Since it is the sport of the national narrative, everyone is expected to excel at it.

I was surprised to find that the bookstore was more like an American university bookstore. I bought Graz sweatshirts, hunter green and white, for Michael and me. I also bought Shakespeare's book of sonnets in English. They didn't carry many American books.

"Roberta told us about your man friend," the lovely Austrian woman said.

"She shouldn't have." I was embarrassed.

"Love is to be celebrated. I could see the sweetness on your face when you were selecting gifts for him."

"He is quite special. I think he wants to go back to America with me," I confessed.

"He's not only special, but smart enough not to let you get away."

My last excursion in Graz was with the American students and my new Austrian friends. We met at the famed Farmer's Market, which was spectacular, even more so than the market in Tübingen with the Greek ladies. Everywhere I looked, I saw the colorful, luscious fruits and vegetables, flowers in the most stunning shades of reds, greens, yellows, and oranges that I could ever imagine. That night, Roberta hosted a huge dinner party at her house. We ate and danced like we had known each other forever. What a send-off!

Leaving Graz, I felt happy and alive. As the train made its way across Austria, I lost myself gazing at the spring snow that had spread across the Alps. Love danced in my heart; I was too excited to sleep, and I didn't want to miss a moment of the magic of such golden grace.

The next morning, I knocked on Bernd Engler's door. "*Kommen Bitte.*"

"Hi, do you have a minute?" I asked.

"Of course I do. How are you? And how was Österreich?" Bernd pointed to a chair.

"It's so beautiful there – a bit on the isolated side, but I had a marvelous time. I brought presents." I handed him a bag containing the famed peanut oil for which Austria is known.

"Well, this was not necessary."

"Of course not, but it was fun. Open it with Lucy tonight. Roberta sends regards."

"Roberta is a good scholar. Too bad about her husband."

"What?"

"He's an excellent scholar and has not been able to find a job. He has become sort of a *Herr Frau*."

"Well, someone has to give up something. He's fortunate to have such a chance to be close to his children," I said.

"But he is the excellent scholar." Bernd Engler tapped his pen on his desk and looked over his glasses. He shook his head of dark and full hair.

"And she was just the good scholar," I persisted.

"That would kill me. I could never have done it."

"You'll be surprised what you can do if necessary. He seemed happy enough to me. I've seen less happy men who are at the top of their game."

"What does that mean?" Bernd Engler asked.

"You know what's interesting about our lives?" I asked, shifting the argument.

"Our lives?" Bernd Engler asked.

"Yours and mine," I smiled. "I am older than you are, but feminism will have no impact on your career."

"Technically, you are the same age if the difference is within two years," he corrected.

"Yeah. Right. I was talking about feminism."

"I know. Not like an American, but feminism will touch my life. Lucy will go back to work, and I do have a daughter, who's on the opinionated side, if you have not noticed."

"That's personal rather than professional."

"But that will have some impact on me."

"Yeah, right. You need to hire a female professor, a real one. But there's something else I need to talk to you about."

"*Bitte*." He looked surprised.

"I've been seeing someone."

"This must be serious, if you're telling me." Bernd raised his eyebrows. "Often, I have to find out what is going on from other sources."

"I think so."

"How long?"

"Let's see; I've been traveling so much it's hard to keep track of time."

"I see. Who is he?"

"His name is Michael Schand. He's finishing up his Ph.D. in physics at Stuttgart this year."

"How old is he?"

"Old enough."

"When are we going to meet him?"

"Soon. I promise, but I've got to go, meeting with a student." I backed out of his office. Now I had told him, and

I knew he would tell Horst Tonn. There was no one else in Germany who needed to know. I felt relieved.

I had organized a series of African American Women Scholars for the department – *African-American Studies Gastvorträge*. Professor Trudier Harris from the University of North Carolina at Chapel Hill was the first to arrive. I had to get everything ready for her visit, but I wanted to see Michael. We talked on the phone every night. It was almost less expensive to take the train to visit him since I had a *Bahn Karte*, which gave me almost a 50% discount on train travel.

Though Michael was sick with a cold, he was still deter-mined to come to Tübingen for the day on Saturday, and he wanted me to go back to Stuttgart with him. That would be a good test. I was moody when I was sick. Maybe he would be angry and whiny. Men could be like that. I would make him tea and be sweet, but not too sweet; I didn't want to spoil him. From what I could tell, German men were spoiled enough.

There is nothing greater than seeing your new lover after being away; the lovemaking is still sweet with newness. I met Michael at the train station. We embraced and walked the half-mile home, only stopping every few minutes for long kisses. He was feeling better. When we got to my house, it was three in the afternoon.

"Can we go to bed?" he asked.

"Yes. Yes." We were so happy, making tender love in the splendor of the afternoon sun. It glowed through my bed-room windows with the angel tree watching over us.

"I don't like being away from you," he said, stroking my left cheek.

"Me either," I reached for his hand. "Just a few more trips. When you're in South Africa, I will go to Berlin and Munich, and then we'll have Prague and Vienna."

"I've been thinking. I want to go back to the States with you right away. This energy we have – it's the real thing." Michael covered me with his warm body. I liked how he made up his mind so matter-of-factly, so unlike a German.

"I would love nothing better, but it would be easier if I went first and got my house in order. It won't be long." I rubbed his back. I had to get my head in order too. My world was about to change in a big way.

"Well, I could go and visit my aunt in New Jersey while you did that. I could also visit Marcus. I want to get to know him on my own."

This man had thought of everything. "That would be nice," I said. What an understatement.

Yes, I was ready. I needed Marcus' input. Boys are never anxious to hand their doting mothers to another man.

"One more thing: I would like for you to come to Celle with me. I want to show you around. You can meet my parents and friends. If we don't do it now, Ethel, I don't know when we'll have time." He held me.

Meeting someone's parents sounded like something my son should be doing. I felt old and odd, but Michael convinced me that his parents were going to love me.

Hunger woke us. We walked the cobblestones streets of Tübingen under a star-lit sky, searching for food.

The next day, I went back to Stuttgart with Michael. Bernd Engler would be arriving the next day to pick up Professor Harris from the airport. I was supposed to go with him, but I didn't feel like explaining to him that I was already there. I thought I would just wait until the morning to call and tell him. Maybe Lucy would answer the phone, and I could give her the message to pass on.

Michael showed me around the *Universität*. We saw a Füssle exhibit at the modern art museum. It wasn't my kind of art, but Füssle was an important artist, a genius. Michael was less impressed than I was.

Though I was having a wonderful time with Michael, I wasn't able to relax until I called Bernd Engler. I didn't want any distractions for the evening.

"Hallo, Ethel. I was just thinking about our trip to the airport."

"Me too. Listen, I am already in Stuttgart. I can just meet you at the airport."

"What are you doing in Stuttgart?" He laughed.

"I'm at Michael's."

"Do you have the information about the flight?"

"Yes. I'll meet you there. It's not that big of an airport."

"Will Michael be there?"

"No, he has a class."

"Have a good evening. It sounds like you will."

"You too."

Michael and I sipped South African wine on his balcony looking onto the coral-brushed sky, hanging as a backdrop for the city of Stuttgart. We were dreaming about our future.

Stuttgart is different from Tübingen, which is less than 30 miles away. It was blown to pieces during the War, but now it has risen from its ashes, much like Atlanta, as a modern city. Stuttgart means horse garden, but it is no longer a garden today; it's grown to be a major metropolitan city, whereas Tübingen is still a medieval town.

"Are we moving too fast?" I asked Michael.

"No. The question is, do you feel sure about us?"

"Yes. I feel like I'm spinning."

"Me too, but that's what the right love will do for you. Spinning is good, Ethel. This will be the spin of your life, darling, the spin of our lives."

I admired and appreciated that Michael appeared to have no doubt. To me, that meant that he was committed. "Have you ever felt like this before?"

"No. Ethel, we can have a good life, a really good life."

"That's what I want Michael, a really good life." We toasted wine to our love. We hoped that it would always be so intoxicating. Our evening ended in the soft glow of the orange evening sky, painting the city in deep corals.

Michael took the train with me to the airport the next morning. I was early, but Bernd Engler was earlier. I found him quickly.

"Good morning," I said. I knew he'd recognize my voice as I approached him. Bernd Engler and Horst Tonn always laughed and said that no one sounded like me.

"Better for some of us than others," Bernd said knowingly.

"Michael really is nice."

"I know, and I am really happy for you. I just like teasing you," Bernd Engler said as he laughed.

"Thanks. We're going to have a party for the 4th of July, and I'm inviting everyone. I think you'll like him."

"Let's have a cup of coffee."

"That's a good idea."

We found a nearby coffee shop and sat down.

"Michael asked me to go to Celle to meet his parents next weekend."

"Meeting a German's parents is a big deal, young lady."

"I know. This is serious."

We saw from the screen that Professor Harris's plane had landed, and we walked to the gate in silence. My life was changing. That was all I could think about. Living with Michael longer would've been helpful. I had just met him. Romance is fabulous, but living together is tough. He was orderly and knew how to take care of himself. German men were well trained in that regard. What would he expect from me? Well, it didn't matter that much since I owned the power of space. Besides, my house is big enough so that we wouldn't get on each other's nerves.

Still, he was the only man I had known who hadn't mentioned another woman or girlfriend by now. Maybe it was cultural. I didn't think I had ever gone out with an American man who hadn't almost immediately started talking about the last woman in his life. Maybe there hadn't been enough time with Michael. I was swirling in a whirlwind of activities, happier than I had ever been with a man. So why was I still so nervous?

I hadn't been back to the States since I left for my Fulbright scholarship, nine months earlier. By avoiding all news,

I was able to keep my head and heart in Germany, just like the immersion German course had taught me to do. Rachel had at least been home a few times since she had a husband waiting for her. Occasionally I heard a sound bite of what was happening in the States. I knew Sony Bono had been killed during a skiing accident. One of the Kennedys died too. There was talk of President Clinton having an affair with an intern. Chelsea Clinton was going to Stanford. Germans laughed at Americans for making national news about a president having an affair. They laughed at us for other reasons, too, like coming to Europe and trying to see it all in ten days. They didn't understand that they were able to travel more due to their holidays, of which we could only dream. Two weeks were all that most of us got. I was grateful for the flexibility of academic life. Other than family and a few friends, I was out of the loop with most of the happenings at home, and I happy to be so.

On the literary front, other than Toni Morrison's new novel *Paradise*, Pulitzer Prize-winning writer James Alan McPherson published his first book of nonfiction, *Crabcakes*. The reviewer from The Washington Post began his critique with, "James Alan McPherson looked 15 years older than he is." The reviewer described himself as a friend. With friends like him, who needs critics?

Everyone was sending me emails and newspaper articles about the new novel by Gayl Jones, *The Healing*. It was her first in twenty years, and she followed it up quickly with another book the next year, *The Mosquito Woman*. Beacon Press published both. At age 26, Gayl Jones had burst onto the literary scene with her first novel, *Corregidora*, published in 1975. Her fame continued with her next novel, *Eva's Man*. She was well known in the American Studies circles of Germany.

In 1983, Gayl Jones moved to Europe in a self-imposed exile. She and her husband, Bob Higgins, had been living in Ann Arbor, Michigan, where she taught. He was a graduate student studying German. From what I understood, Higgins appeared at a Gay Rights Rally and shouted something about AIDS and going to hell. A fight broke out. He left, but when he returned with a shotgun, he was arrested. Gayl Jones resigned her position by sending a letter to President Reagan and a copy to the university president, stating that she rejected their racism and was calling on God. Afterwards, they left the country and lived in Paris.

When Newsweek published a story about her latest novel, the police tracked her husband down since there was a warrant out for his arrest. Bob Higgins tried to kill Gayl, but he was unsuccessful. He then killed himself by slicing his throat. Gayl was admitted to an asylum and remains there as far as I know. Her life seemed more like the fiction she wrote.

Before I could continue my thoughts of home, Trudier Harris, a friend and colleague, was standing before us. We are Wintergreen sisters, a group of mostly Black women in the academic world who meet once a year for a retreat in Wintergreen, Virginia, and other places. At this writing, we have been retreating for more than 20 years now. How wonderful it was to see a friend from home.

We drove from the airport with Trudier doing most of the talking, telling us about her other travels. She had been in England before arriving in Germany. Trudier liked the driving in Germany. She was more of a driver than me. Since I was sitting in the back seat, it was easy to disengage. I was glad to be sitting in the back; Bernd Engler drives too fast. I often thought I was going to throw up while riding with him. Germans were quite fond of their cars.

I thought of Michael. Had I ever been in love before? What would we fight about? Life wouldn't be so blissful all the time. What is under the romance? Could I live with him? He felt so right. It was like shopping for a pair of shoes; when you find the ones that fit just right and look great, you don't even have to look at the price tag to know that you're going to buy them. He had given us a lot of thought. I was beginning to feel like Michael and I could have a good life together, a really good life. I felt connected to this intelligent and handsome man. He had the ability to love without being afraid. Was he too handsome? Would his flirting get on my nerves? No, it had actually encouraged me to flirt too. Thinking of Michael made it easy for me to smile through the evening activities.

Lucy, always the gracious host, had cooked a delicious dinner. Lucy and Ursula were the best cooks in Tübingen. After dinner, Trudier and I went back to my flat.

"Girl, I'd need a car if I lived here," Trudier said as we trudged along.

"I'm glad not to have a car. It would be just one more hassle."

By this time, I had an answering machine, and I had even recorded my greeting in German, though it had taken five attempts before it was intelligible. Michael had said that my German was excellent. I knew he was lying, but I liked it anyway. He often complained that Germans in the South spoke horribly. Often while dining at a restaurant, Michael would turn to me and ask what the waiter had said. We always laughed.

Two messages blinked on my answering machine. Both were from Michael, telling me how wonderful the weekend had been and that he was looking forward to spending the rest of his life having wonderful weekends with me. The other message was a P.S. to the first message.

I played the messages five times with excitement. I was so in love.

Professor Harris' talk was titled, "What Women? What Canon? – African American Women and the Literary Canon" She proclaimed that none of the African American women writers had even been to Africa. My students had a good time. Afterwards, Bernd Engler and the other professors took us out to dinner.

Two days later, we drove her back to the airport in Stuttgart. I took my overnight bag and went to Michael's as soon as we got to the airport. I should have stayed with my guest until she boarded the plane, but I was in love.

The next Tuesday, a train derailed 20 miles south of Celle in the town of Eschede: the worst in the history of the train system, killing more than 100 people. The ICE high speed

Wilhelm Conrad Röntgen was on route from Munich to Hamburg when a broken wheel caused the disaster. Since Michael's father had worked with the *Bahn* system, he was able to get information that wasn't available to the general public. For example, he told us that there had been 50 garbage bags of body parts. I was sick to my stomach when I heard that. It's all Michael and I were talking about.

We weren't alone, though. Everyone was talking about the accident. Bernd Engler and Horst Tonn said Michael and I should postpone our trip. We didn't have time. Our schedules were packed. There was no room for the slightest change. Michael was leaving for South Africa the next week, and then I was headed to Munich. Then we would be off to Prague and Vienna. After that, it would be time for me to start preparing to go back to the States. I didn't want to think. It was all too much. Could I get ready this quickly? What if something went wrong with Michael? Would I ever sleep again? I had to take some chances if I wanted to change my life to include a romantic partner.

We learned our trip to Celle could be up to two hours late, since the *Bahn* system had to reroute trains around the derailment. I said to Michael that I didn't understand what the big deal was. We'd just prepare for the trip by playing games and talking. Somehow, the tardiness of the trains offended the Germans. It was not just an inconvenience; it was a betrayal. Something they had built and counted on had failed them. If Michael was going to get so upset about the train being late, could he handle the racism in the States? Did he have any idea how his life was going to be because of me? He could have a simpler life with someone else, not a Black woman.

Celle has 700 years of lively history. The closed historic town center has timbered-style houses from the 16th, 17th, and 18th centuries. According to Michael, tradition and open-mindedness have shaped the culture of this unique city. Hotels are charming, and cafés are lovely. Cozy wine cellars and restaurants of international and national specialties lined the streets. Celle looked like a postcard, as so many places in Germany did.

Though Michael always wanted to be tied to Celle, he wanted to live in other places like South Africa and America. He even wanted a summer place on the white beaches of Dresden. I liked a man with big dreams, but I couldn't imagine how he would have time to live in all of those places. What was the cost of maintaining such a lifestyle? Did he have more money than I thought? I had dreams, too, in the form of a brownstone in Boston and a summer place on Martha's Vineyard. I could even live in another country. I didn't know for how long, but I had lived in Germany for nearly a year and felt no real desire to leave. Yet, I knew the time would come when I would feel the call of home.

When we finally arrived, Michael showed me around, expressing passion and excitement about his hometown. I couldn't relate. I hated rural Alabama; if you're a little Black girl with dreams, it's just a place you dream of escaping. I only went back to visit my mother and sisters. I would never experience such an emotion about land.

I tried to show appreciation for his energetic spirit, but after seeing every castle and cathedral of note during my year in Europe, I was having a difficult time feeling excitement about one more German town. Plus, I was exhausted from not only a lack of sleep, but also all of the emotion in my life. The train wreck had added another level of stress. If you're not sleeping, excitement is the first thing to go. I knew that if I could just sleep for one complete night, I would shift into a better gear.

I was disappointed that I couldn't buy flowers for Michael's mother; the train station shops were closed since it was late Saturday afternoon when we arrived. Greeting a future mother-in-law with flowers is a good way to say hello. I felt nervous and stressed, empty without a bouquet. Michael had told me on the train that I should only speak German to his mother if I wanted her to understand me. This was going to be a disaster. Could I do this? I should have been studying German on the long and exhausting train ride. To told myself to calm down; Michael would be there to translate.

In a new relationship, you have no reference or background with the person. I didn't know how Michael handled pressure or how we'd deal with any problems during the visit. I was seeing no in-between with Michael's personality. Everything was either absolutely great or awful. He was so serious when telling me to speak German to his mother. What he should've said was, "I am here with you, beside you." Also, the lingering problem in the back of my mind was how, when he spoke about an issue, it would be over: the end, no further discussion necessary. He was testing the wrong woman. Life had demanded that I speak up for myself. I wasn't about to pass my power over to him like it was a side dish of *Sauerkraut*.

Michael's parents were friendly and happy to see me. His mother cooked a splendid meal of white asparagus and a light steamed fish; it wasn't familiar to me, but it tasted delicious. The anticipation of the season of white asparagus had arrived in Germany like a new baby. Other than the train accident, the spring crop of asparagus was on everyone's lips. Asparagus have some kind of sexual connotation for Germans. I never had time to ask, but once I was back in the States, I saw it referenced in a film, *The Comedian Harmonist*.

I liked Michael's mother. She walked with the grace of a dancer, dignified like Helen, my hair braider. I complimented her on her warm and wonderful house. There were photos of Michael everywhere, and I enjoyed watching him grow up through photos: long hair, big glasses, and shy smiles. After we washed dishes, she showed me her garden of beautiful vegetables. I could live with her as a mother-in-law. My German would improve, and I would teach her English.

Later, I heard her on the telephone telling someone that Michael had brought an American college professor home. She sounded proud, but I thought that Michael surely must have brought a girlfriend home before.

Michael's father spoke some English, thankfully. I told them the one joke I knew how to tell in German.

"What's a German without guilt? An Italian." Everyone always laughed, although I didn't know why. Since it was high Deutsch, their German was easier for me to understand, yet I was still disappointed that Michael wasn't helping me. I thought it might be his silly way of testing for me. His father talked about visiting his sister in Florida, how they would surely visit us. That sounded nice to me. We were officially a couple, an *us*. Had Michael told me earlier that I was going to have to speak to his mother in German, I would have brought my German/English dictionary, my Bible. Why hadn't I thought to bring such a sacred book?

When I asked them if they had a *Stadtplan*, a map, they obliged me. I showed them where I lived, where I was born, and where I had gone to school. I didn't mention Marcus. Michael's parents and I were engaging. His father showed me where they had traveled in the States and Canada. I then showed them the areas I had explored in Germany and Austria. Michael seemed pleased that I had figured out a way to communicate with his parents without his help. We all relaxed. Everyone was smiling. We were an *us*. I felt like they approved. They understood my German, at least enough for us to share our experiences and connect. I remembered Silvia saying, "It's the key words."

I was surprised and disappointed to know that I would be sleeping in the guest room, alone. I had been looking forward to sleeping with Michael, not so much for sex but for comfort, to calm me down into sleep. Instead, I slept in the pleasant guest room and tried to read. Germans prized themselves on being open and honest about sex. It seemed odd that a 36-year-old man who would travel across the sea and into another country for this woman would not be sleeping with her. I was sure they knew I wasn't a virgin. But it was their house, and I respected their rules.

The next morning, I woke up to the sound of birds singing. I had slept so well that I didn't even mind getting up early. Already, I was in a better mood. After breakfast, we spent a stress-free day with his oldest friends, whom I had met earlier in Stuttgart. Even though Michael was attentive – calling me 'sweetheart' and all of his other pet names for me – I felt his distance. I thought maybe it had to do with me being nervous. The harder I tried to relax, the more nervous I felt.

Michael's bachelor friend, a high school physics teacher, invited us for cocktails and dinner the following evening. I was sure I wasn't making the best impression; I was tired and weary, but I felt good since everyone seemed warmer than I had expected. I could tell that they loved Michael. His oldest friend told me that Michael was happier than he had ever seen him. That calmed me down some.

The next day, Saturday, we took the train to Hamburg, where Michael's favorite college professor was throwing a party in our honor. I felt like we were moving as fast as the ICE trains, but our closeness was slipping off track. Maybe it was because of the sleeping arrangement, or maybe we were around each other too much. In real life, we would have more of our own space. There were too many thoughts, too many emotions, for me to sort them all. I wasn't about to make any rash decisions about my love life in an exhausted state of mind.

In Hamburg, we spent the night with a former roommate. At least we would be sleeping together, but the sleeping arrangements turned out to be on the floor: a mattress, more of a pad, which hurt my back. When I couldn't sleep, I got angry and asked Michael why didn't we reserve a room at a hotel. He said it was too expensive. "I am a college professor. I would've been happy to pay for a room," I spat out.

Finally, I was on my way back to Tübingen. Michael continued on to see some of his relatives in the former East, and I wouldn't hear from him for almost three weeks. Our goodbye had been hurried because of all of the chaos at the train stations. Germans don't function well outside of order. I didn't think that it was the end of the world because the trains were late. Just read or write in your journal. These folks wouldn't function well in New York City.

I was surprised that no one was talking about the real sadness: the poor folks whose chopped up body parts were in body bags. Instead, the conversation revolved around their disbelief and shock that one of their trains had derailed, and the white asparagus crop. Perhaps I didn't have much appreciation for their culinary delights, but I didn't think white asparagus tasted that different from the green ones I ate at home. Maybe it was because, to Germans, everything is pretty much the same: boil it until it's white. I had eaten at many dinners where all of the food was white.

On the train home, I was alone. I could think for the first time in a long time. I felt troubled, but I didn't understand why. Everyone had been friendly and made an effort to welcome me. My trouble wasn't with Michael's family or friends, but with Michael. I needed sleep, but I was afraid that I would miss an announcement about a train schedule and end up in the former East. I had more questions about Michael than answers. I needed to talk to him. It hadn't been a bad trip – rushed, but not bad.

Michael has a short attention span, I was learning. He seemed more childish than he had earlier. I felt that, in order to stay in each other's worlds, we had to be together. What an odd conclusion. I had no reason for why I reached such a conclusion. Maybe that was the boy in Michael. He could be so serious about his career or a book of poetry, yet so boyish when it came to life. At least I was learning something about him. The question was, after learning what I had about him, could I live peacefully with myself? With him?

Back in Tübingen, my classes were buzzing about the talk Professor's Trudier gave. Our next speakers would arrive in two weeks. Professor Karla Holloway from Duke University was going to talk about her book-in-progress, *African-American Mourning Stories*, and Professor Joyce Pettis from North Carolina State University would deliver a talk titled, "African-American Fiction and the Festive Enterprise." I was looking forward to their visits as well. The universe was sending me lovely notes from home.

I resumed my German classes with Silvia. We had worked out her childcare problem in America. Since her oldest son, Dave, would be a senior, he would stay with Klaus. Jonas would go with her. They had even found a school for him.

I tried not to talk about Michael, but I thought about him all the time. I sent his mother flowers, a difficult task in Germany. We had taken flowers to his high school teacher and his professor's houses, and I wrote them thank you notes too.

I had another outing with GAWC. Everyone was talking about Michael and me. The mentor had told Ulli that Michael was happier than he had ever known him to be. They all would be invited to the wedding.

"Wait," I raised my hand. "We're getting ahead of ourselves."

"Yes, we know." Ulli laughed her music.

The next day, I was working in my office when my telephone rang.

"Are you sitting down?" Rachel asked.

"Yes. Should I be?"

"Klaus and I are getting a divorce." She said it as though she was asking me what I had eaten for lunch.

"I'm so sorry."

"It's really okay. We've been through this, and there is no other way."

"What about your holiday in Bali?"

"Once we made a decision to get divorced, we had a great time."

"Rachel, this can't be easy."

"Klaus is a very difficult man to live with. The divorce will be easier than you can imagine. What did you think I was going to say to you?"

"Well, I thought you were going to tell me you were pregnant or getting a divorce," I admitted.

"You know me well." We tried to laugh.

"I'm here for you, Rachel."

"How's your love life?"

I gave her all of the updates, then asked, "Rachel, do you think we're moving too fast?"

"You know, Ethel, it doesn't matter if you go too fast, too slow, or somewhere in the middle; either it works or it doesn't. Michael sounds great and madly in love with you. Are you in love with him? That's the question. But girlfriend, if you don't know, you can have one helluva of a time finding out."

"I think so. Love is such fickle business," I said.

"That's why it's love."

"He takes my breath away. I wish I knew something about his other girlfriends, though."

"In the world of relationships, even that doesn't mean a whole lot."

"I know. I am just looking for some sort of comfort."

"A lot has happened to you in the last few weeks. Just see if you can enjoy and not worry. You'll know soon enough," Rachel offered.

"Thanks, girlfriend."

"Remember, I'll be there next week."

"That's right. We're going to have a good time. Don't think I'll be having a bad German day for a while," I said, looking forward to seeing my friend.

"We'll never be the same after this experience."

"Well said."

"Bye, sweetheart. I'll email you my agenda. And remember, I am here for you."

"And that I find comforting." We giggled.

I was disappointed that there was no note or card from Michael among my mail that day. I was used to receiving notes and cards from him at least twice a week. Feeling unsettled, I tried to remember that he was in South Africa, which probably meant slower mail.

I always told my class where I was traveling. Their input could be helpful. By this time, I had traveled farther and wider than many of my students had done. They were impressed that I had just come from Berlin, but curious to know why I was going to Munich.

"Well, I was invited, and I accepted. It's a famous place, one I've never seen before."

"Professor Smith, there is a rivalry between us and Bavaria," a student informed me.

"Really?"

"You have to remember, Bavaria didn't want to be part of Germany," the same student continued to teach me about the intrastate enmity.

"Why?"

"Because they're special."

"And you hold that against them?" I asked.

"Yes, because they still think they're special."

"I see. Well, I'll keep that in mind," I promised.

My trip to Munich was as uneventful as my students had predicted, and it was the least friendly of the places I had visited. After giving to more than 20 lectures around Germany and Austria, it was hard to be energetic. I wanted this part of my Fulbright experience to be over. I hoped Michael was just as anxious to get back to me as I was to return to him.

Back in Tübingen, I wanted to be ready for Michael. Helen braided my hair. I cleaned my flat and washed my laundry. While I prepared myself for his arrival, I had time to think and reflect. What we had done in such a short period of time was hard. I was excited and nervous to see him again, to be together at a slower pace.

Two days had passed since Michael had told me he would be back, yet I hadn't heard from him. I didn't want to feel insecure, a very unattractive trait for any woman. It wasn't urgent enough to call Ulli. I thought, maybe he's totally exhausted, got in late and went to sleep. Too soon to start worrying. Maybe I had gotten the days mixed up with the time change. I could certainly have been wrong about the date; after not communicating for three weeks, my memory wasn't quite clear.

About once a month, I went shopping with the Englers to a large grocery store. Their grocery shopping was more of an old-fashioned outing, typical of the 1950s in America. On this day, I happily sat in the backseat with their children, Toby and Dorothy.

I strolled through the market aisles looking for candles, peanut butter, yogurt, bath products, toilet paper, paper towels, detergents, and other items that were too heavy for me to carry from the *Stadt*. The Englers devoted a day to shopping. Who had that kind of time in the States? But shopping together wasn't a bad outing. Lucy didn't have to lug everything, which I did a lot of in Germany. It was important to be in good shape. I walked, ran down trains, and lugged food, flowers, and wine up the hill. On top of that, I hiked and played tennis.

I walked around, throwing items in my cart. Bernd Engler followed behind me, stacking my food orderly. "It drives me crazy that you do that," I said.

"It drives me crazy that you just throw the food in the cart," Bernd Engler said.

This was an ongoing disagreement between us. Lucy and the children always laughed. This would be the last time I would be shopping with the Englers. Change was coming at me fast.

At the checkout, Bernd Engler paid for their food with cash. Germans carried lots of cash. Unlike Americans, who never had any; at least that was true for my world. I joked with my students that I should go around and rob people; I'd make a fortune. I can remember a time when, having forgotten to go to the bank, I was out of cash in Frankfurt. Bernd Engler offered to lend me money and asked how much I needed.

"Five hundred," I said, and he pulled out his wallet and gave me the money on the spot. It didn't even empty his full wallet.

"Why do you have so much money?" I asked.

"This isn't so much money," he laughed. "We just have to be ready."

In Germany, you couldn't just assume you could charge your dinner at a restaurant, unless perhaps you were in a major city. Germans don't use credit cards as frequently as Americans. They are more of a cash-and-carry bunch. Bernd Engler said they only went in debt for a house and sometimes a car. When they did use their charge cards, they paid them off at the end of the month, similar to our debit cards. Although Germans do borrow from their *Kontos*, it's nothing like the debt Americans rack up.

After I got home late that afternoon, I decided to call Michael. I didn't think he would be at home. If he had been, surely he would have called me.

"Hallo," he answered.

"Hi, Michael. It's Ethel," I said, trying to the shock from my voice. I'd only planned to leave a message on the machine. Now, hearing his voice, I felt nervous. Had he been ignoring me?

"Hi, Ethel. I was going to call you."

"When did you get home?"

"Two days ago." Something was wrong. I heard doom in his distant voice.

"How was your trip?" I thought if I just kept talking, I would know what was happening.

"Wonderful, the most amazing trip of my life."

"Good. What did you do?"

"Look, Ethel. I met someone else. I am in love with her. We spent the whole two weeks together."

"What?"

"I am sorry to have to tell you like this, but you need to know."

I reeled in disbelief. I had to sit down. I was sick to my stomach.

"You heard me right," he said coldly.

"What about us?" I shook.

"There was never *us*. You're too serious about your career, way too serious about everything. Being away from you gave me the perspective I needed." His voice was even. It was as though he was telling me what he ate for breakfast.

"What are you talking about?" If only we could just talk reasonably, I kept thinking. How could this be happening?

"Trust me, you'll get over it. I had a girlfriend. Five years ago, she went on holiday for two weeks to New Zealand. When she came back, she told me she had been on holiday with her new lover."

"What does this have to do with me?"

"I was just using it as an example. I can't talk to you anymore. I am waiting for a phone call from South Africa."

"You can just do this?"

"Do what? Fall in love?"

I hung up the telephone. Feeling numb, I sat on my sofa. I wished I could call someone. I wished there was a pill I could take. I wished I could die. What had I not understood? What clue had I not read? Damn! Damn! Damn this monster of a man! Was this a mean trick? I took off my clothes, slipped between my sheets, and prayed there was no scent of him left in my bed.

Chapter 7

ICH BIN EIN BERLINER

The heart of a woman falls back with the night,
And enters some alien cage in its plight,
And tries to forget it has dreamed of the stars,
While it break, break, breaks, on the sheltering bars.

- Georgia Douglas Johnson

At about nine that evening, my telephone rang. I thought I heard bells, but I knew not to trust myself. Half asleep, I answered the telephone, thinking it was Michael calling to apologize, or perhaps to awake me from the nightmare I had just experienced. Nothing made any sense. And what if he were calling to apologize? The damage had already been done. He had shot a hole through my heart.

"Hallo, Ethel. It's Rosemarie."

"Hi, how are you?"

"You sound awful. I've had two dreams about you and was beginning to worry."

"Rosemarie." I couldn't get another word out before bursting into tears.

"What's wrong?"

I told her the whole story, what Michael had said to me. She was gracious enough to allow me to cry.

"Oh, Ethel, this makes no sense to me. He has taken you home to meet his parents, his teachers and his friends. How can he just do this?"

"Rosemarie, I did not pursue him in the least. He just came into my life and swept me into this fantasyland."

"I will take the earliest train to Tübingen tomorrow. We'll hike all day, then have a nice dinner. That'll help get the bastard out of your system."

"He is a bastard, isn't he?" I repeated. The worst kind of bastard waltzed into my life and turned it upside down. That was exactly what he had done, but I sure had made it easy for him. Damn! Damn! Damn! Why had I believed him? Would a more experienced woman have believed him? Why wouldn't I have believed him? He was sincere, serious – smooth as Marzipan.

I hung up the telephone and walked into the bathroom. I blew my nose, then ran a tub of hot water. While the water ran, I brewed a pot of black tea. I did feel better after telling someone else; at least Rosemarie hadn't thought I was the fool I felt like. Egos are as fragile as tea leaves. I prized myself on having common sense and being practical. My accomplishments hadn't happened because of me being foolish.

I gathered all of Michael's letters and cards and reread them in the bath. He had written me too much; it had always made me suspicious. I didn't have time to write love notes twice a week, especially since we talked on the telephone every night. It was flattering in the beginning, but he had done it so much that it didn't mean anything. Had I missed another clue? Well, to be honest, he did all the writing trying to impress me, the writer. I didn't want to be impressed, nor did I want broken promises. I wanted to get to know him, the real Michael. I wondered if he knew the real Michael.

Even if he had fallen in love with someone else, I was leaving in less than two months. Two goddamn months! No, six weeks. Six goddamn weeks! Couldn't he have let time and distance end the relationship? Why had he needed to hurt me? Was he getting back at me for being dumped by an old girlfriend all those years ago? My intuition had been right about him: not mentioning a girlfriend was a sign of trouble. I was searching for answers to questions I didn't know. Was he happy after being so cruel to me? What kind of monster was he? All of the letters were full of hope and love. God, I hated him.

Rosemarie embraced me at the train station the following morning, which surprised me. I hadn't thought of her as the nurturing type.

"I am so tired of crying. Thank you so much for coming." I wondered, were my tears really for Michael or about what could have been? Had I been in love with him? Was I still? I always thought that in order to be in love, you had to grow in love. There hadn't been time for anything other than being shocked off of my feet. Even after figuring this out, I still couldn't stop crying.

"I am glad that I was in town." Rosemarie threw up her hands. "I could feel that something was wrong."

Rosemarie knew Tübingen well. We hiked to the top of the famed *Würmlinger Kapelle*. I was hoping to see a rainbow, which is a comma sight at the *Kapelle*. After an hour, we stopped at a winery for tea and cake. "I've found that talking about men can be the best medicine," Rosemarie said.

"I don't have a lot of experience, but I'm not crazy," I said.

"Men can play with your head." Rosemarie pointed toward her head.

"I just feel like such a fool. I know he did the wooing, but I bought the Kool-Aid, and it tasted so good." I burst into tears again. I didn't want to cry for such a jerk. I couldn't remember the last time I had cried over a man. That's what teenagers and silly women did.

"That doesn't give him permission to use you. And who falls in love in two weeks?"

"Michael. I am afraid he did the same thing with me. Damnit, he's one of those fall-deep-fast kind of guys. That's the easy stuff."

"Does he have money?" Rosemarie asked.

"We never talked about it. I thought when he got a job in the States, we would work out a budget."

"You mean money didn't come up once?"

"No." I stabbed the *Stollen* with my fork.

"Always get the money worked out. You can learn a lot about a man that way. I am sure his parents have money."

"They seemed settled, owning their own home. I didn't have enough time to figure everything out."

"Always find out where the money is coming from."

"Did I tell you about the time he graced my flat with lilacs?"

"What do you mean?"

"One day, I came home, and lilacs were everywhere, all over my flat in every room. It was quite beautiful."

"Does he have a key?"

"No, he talked the cleaning lady into letting him in. She was there the whole time."

"How did you feel?"

"That I was being wooed." I shrugged my shoulders, continuing, "And there was a letter that said he could never think about lilacs without thinking about how we met in Haigerloch."

"That is romantic."

"But it's easy, if you think about it."

"Who cares? He's no one for you. Not dependable."

"I thought German men were dependable."

"Dependability isn't something that comes in countries. That's like saying African Americans have rhythm."

"I know that. I'm sorry," I said, thinking of all my recent mistakes. "What a fool I've been."

"It's never foolish to fall in love."

Rosemarie and I continued to sit in the glow of the spring sun, smearing the name of Michael Schand, just like good girlfriends do when one of their own has been wounded.

"I have an idea." Rosemarie sipped her tea, her blonde hair shining in the splendor of the sun.

"What?" I asked.

"Let's talk about all of the things you didn't like about him."

"First, we won't call him by his name," I said. "What should we call him? What's low enough for him?"

Rosemarie thought for a second, then said, "*Betrug*. It means cheater in German."

"Yes, that's perfect! Rosemarie, how do you know so much about getting over men?"

"Practice. And more practice. Too much practice, I'm afraid." We laughed.

"The first thing is that he was either funny or cruel, but in a passive aggressive kind of way," I recounted. "I'm not used to mean people, at least not in my immediate life. I didn't feel that way until our trip to Celle. I could never live like that."

"How did he act around his parents?"

"They didn't seem that close. They acted formally around each other. If I didn't know better, I'd think he was jealous that they liked me. But I don't know their history." I bit into my *Stollen*.

"How?"

"They seemed like nice enough people, really. Michael acted odd, though. For one thing, he didn't participate in the conversations, especially not when I was talking, and even less when I tried to speak German. It wasn't like he helped me with my German, either. I tried so hard, and I think his parents understood me, especially his father. I found ways to communicate with his mother. She showed me her garden, and I could speak to her in German about flowers. I helped her with the dishes, and we smiled a lot. I told her that Michael looked like her. I thought he would have been impressed by how I handled our differences.

"He didn't help you at all?" Rosemarie was shocked, "I think he should have prepared you more for this trip. You walked into a disaster!"

"Yeah, I wish he'd at least prepped me for the language difference or offered his help when his parents and I struggled. I was so nervous; I could've done better on my own."

"He didn't help you at all?" Rosemarie was shocked.

"No, I felt like I was involved in some kind of game, but I didn't know the rules. It wasn't like that with his friends; they spoke English. I had already met one couple before in Stuttgart."

"What else didn't you like about him?" Rosemarie was good at probing me for details, and by letting me talk, she was showing me what I already knew, but hadn't yet admitted: I was better off without *Betrug*.

"He got on my nerves by thinking I should have a favorite book, or a favorite poet, or a favorite something or other. I don't have favorite things, especially not books. I love many movies, many poems, and many, many books. So childish."

"That's what you do, though. Your work revolves around books, and he thinks you can chose one over them all? Absurd. How could he not understand?"

"I didn't like it that he thought he could discuss Toni Morrison with me after only reading one of her novels, *Sula*. I don't mean talking about the novel, but Morrison as a writer and her scholarship about her writing. I wanted to talk more about German writers, with whom he surely was more familiar. Rosemarie, he read poetry to me." I covered my face with both hands and choked back tears.

"That sounds romantic."

"At least it was German poetry. It could be romantic, but it felt phony. He's no poet. It was all just part of his act, anyway." I flicked my fork in the air.

"I see, but I have to admit: I would have been swept off my feet, too, as you say. He wouldn't discuss German writers with you? I would, gladly!"

"I've been reading W.G. Sebald. Do you know his work?"

"No. He's new on the German scene."

"He's mainly known for *The Emigrants*. That was the first of his books I read. *The Rings of Saturn* and *Vertigo* are others. What about Wolfgang Borchert? On our first real date, *Betrug* gave me some short stories by him."

"He's not so well-known. What did you think of his writing?"

"I was only interested because of *Betrug's* love of the work. I don't actually remember any of them."

"I know what you mean," Rosemarie said. "You wanted to learn more about his culture."

"Yes, exactly," I agreed. "If he's in love with literature, then I want to know who or what influenced him."

"I think you'll like Christa Wolf's work," Rosemarie suggested. "Do you know about her?"

"No, but I'm already looking forward to reading her books."

"She's from the former East. She also wrote *Kassandra, Patterns of Childhood, What Remains, Parting From Phantoms,* and *The Quest for Christa T.*

"I can't wait to read some other women writers from here."

"It's important to understand each other's' art and culture. Reading is the best way to do that."

"Who are some of the African writers you studied at Amherst?"

"Chinua Achebe, of course."

"He's pretty global. What about women?"

"Ama Ata Aidoo and Bessie Head."

"I know their work. They're fabulous writers," I agreed. Our conversation was so easy and natural, suggesting new writers and critiquing others.

"Thank you so much for coming, Rosemarie. I couldn't have made it without you." I felt engaged with my friend, and I forgot about myself. The sun was falling through the trees, splashing above Rosemarie's blonde hair.

"Yes, you would have, but it's better to have some support."

"To friendship." I raised my glass.

"To friendship and literature." Rosemarie raised her glass.

I felt stronger and thankful after Rosemarie left. I had stopped crying and had started to think. I still had to get through this Fulbright. Damn him! Damn him! He wasn't going to ruin it for me. I'm not some flake or some man-crazy babe, either. I am sensible and responsible; I deserved closure. Rosemarie had given me some good ideas.

So I called.

"We need to talk," I began. "I can understand you meeting someone, but that's no reason to be so venomous toward me. I haven't done anything to you." I spoke with a steady voice.

"It's important that you have no hope that we'll ever get back together," he spat into the telephone.

"How can you be like this?" I asked. "Can't we just meet to say goodbye? This is no way to end." Complete silence shot through my heart. Cars zoomed outside of my window.

"We meant something to each other, right?" I continued. What would he say to his parents, his friends and professors who had welcomed me into their lives? They spoke of how happy he was. I wished I could talk to them. What would they say to me?

"This is just who I am. It does not help to prolong such matters."

"You don't feel any sense of responsibility?"

"I love her, you know."

"You loved me three weeks ago."

"That is not the point."

"What is the point?"

"I don't want to see you again," he growled through the phone.

I hung up the telephone. No one had ever told me that they never wanted to see me again. His words struck the center of my soul like enemy bullets, but I had to keep living.

There had been no break-up with Helmut, my German boyfriend in the States. He simply had to leave for home. Though it was clear that we would never see each other again, our relationship grew complicated the longer he delayed his return to Germany. Even though we had lived in domestic bliss, the deal was the same. How I appreciated his honesty.

I pulled myself up from my bed and listened to the richness of Dinah Washington's voice singing "No Time For Tears." I knew I would survive as I sipped Chianti in my backyard. I asked the angel tree, how could this be the man who had all of the answers for the rest of our lives? He had convinced me that we were going to live the "really good life." Was this the man who loved Marc Chagall? How could this poet of a man perpetrate such an act of tyranny against my heart?

The next week, I walked around in befuddlement, unable to believe what had happened. Silvia was in the States. I missed her but would not bother her. She was trying to adjust in a new place, and her father was ailing. I kept reminding myself that I just had a few more weeks. Anna, a colleague and friend from home, was coming to Stuttgart for a conference. Afterwards, she would come to Tübingen to help me pack, the start of my journey home.

After her visit, I was going to Greece with Silvia and Klaus. From there, I would meet Marcus in Edinburgh, Scotland, for a music festival. Time was on my side. If I could just get home, in my house, to sleep in my bed, in my safe and limited world, I could start over again. If I could just play tennis and have my book club over for lunch, my life would be fine. If I could just be in my house, a space that he had never spoiled.

Two weeks after I telephoned *Betrug*, I received a telephone call from the University of Missouri Press. They wanted to publish my book on Hollins College. Just like that, my life changed. I was thrilled, and so was everyone else in Brecht Hall. Bernd Engler, Horst Tonn, and my other colleagues committed themselves to helping me get whatever the publisher needed. This was no small feat. Since I hadn't expected the book to be accepted for publication, I wasn't sure if I had all of my files. Bernd Engler and Horst Tonn made fun of me having such disorganized files. They even suggested that I write a book telling writers what not to do.

A few days after the acceptance of the manuscript, I panicked. After so many years of being rejected, could I actually complete the work? I had begun to think that I would never get the book published since it had been rejected so many times. Did I have enough of my files or other resources here? All of my friends were telling me that I could get this work done. I wasn't panicky around Bernd Engler and Horst Tonn. When they were around, I felt like I could get the work done because we were actually doing the work. Germans are proactive when it comes to work, or maybe I was experiencing feminism. There were men to save me. No wonder I hadn't thought much about feminism at home: no one saved me.

For the first time in weeks, I wasn't thinking or paining over *Betrug*. I threw myself into the project, working day and night. It pleased everyone that they didn't have to talk or be reminded of *Betrug*, who had hurt and embarrassed Ulli and all of my other friends. Their hurt was not like mine, but as Germans. I suffered from the hollows of my heart, and they suffered from the betrayal of a countryman.

With so much excitement about the acceptance of my manuscript, I had forgotten that Professors Karla Holloway and Joyce Pettis were to arrive soon. I was motivated to work even harder on my book. I was looking forward to their visit, knowing they would be great guests.

One of my guests from Seattle was angry when she arrived because it snowed three inches. She kept screaming; she was on her spring holiday, and this wasn't the kind of weather she wanted. I had to finally tell her that I wasn't in charge of the weather. She never cleaned the bathroom or washed a dish, although she complained when a spoon wasn't clean enough for her. I told her to wash it.

Students were excited. Professor Holloway was going to read from her work-in-progress, and Professor Pettis was going to present her work on the author Paule Marshall for my afternoon seminar. I cleaned my flat, shopped, and organized my office. Twin beds occupied my bedroom, and the sofa made a bed in the living room. Even though there was only one bathroom, if I took a bath at night, we would manage fine.

Bernd Engler and I drove to the Stuttgart airport, happy to be talking about my manuscript and the activities he had planned for Karla and Joyce. My German colleagues treated guests like royalty. I felt like I was more than a visitor. They had rallied around me and protected me from one of their own. What a powerful moment of global grace. I had entertained many guests during my time in Germany, I was far closer to Karla and Joyce. Traveling with someone is a test of a sort. You learn quickly if you will or won't do it again.

I had asked Karla and Joyce to bring me a pair of black spring gloves and new soft toothbrushes. I never saw a soft toothbrush in Germany. I had been invited to serve on a panel for the USIA in Bonn, and I would also be one of the readers after the formal dinner. It would be the last event before the USIA moved to Berlin. I wanted to look good while making history. Once, I had tried to shop for clothes in Strasbourg, but the cut of the French and Italian clothes was a no no-no on my hips. I had better luck with make-up, finding Fashion Fair cosmetics, which I had never seen in Morgantown or Pittsburgh.

My flat sang with laughter and chatter. Luggage, boxes, and purses were everywhere. Karla, Joyce, and I were sipping Prosecco, which become their favorite before the trip was over.

"To friendship!" I said, but in the excitement, I caught myself slipping into a cry. "I can't believe you're here." My tears were of joy and gratitude. True friends had come such a long way to see me, and they were genuinely interested in my life.

"It would've never occurred to me to come to Germany," Karla said.

"Me either," Joyce added.

"Well, it's great here. The best thing is that everyone wants to know what they can do for me," I said.

"I could live with that," Joyce said.

"Black women in America should come to Europe," I said.

"Why?" Karla asked.

"You'll see yourself differently living here."

"How?"

"We are beautiful!"

"I thought it was exotic," Joyce said.

"Same thing," I answered.

"How did your department react about you getting the award?" Karla asked.

"Well, not as congratulatory as you might think. Even my chair tried to downplay the significance. He told me that Fulbrights weren't nearly as prestigious as they used to be. Apparently, almost everyone gets them these days.'"

"Get out of here," Joyce said.

"What did you say to him?" Karla asked.

"I asked if that was congratulations."

"What did he say?"

"Nothing. He just dwelled on the fact that I had to go through procedures from the Dean's office. He hoped I understood that I couldn't just up and leave without permission."

"Did you say, 'Yessir, Mr. Charlie?'" Karla asked.

"I wanted to ask where he had spent his Fulbright, but I didn't want to act like a real colored babe." We laughed again and again.

"Here's to when a Fulbright isn't a Fulbright." Karla raised her glass, and we followed. "Opal has a poem, or maybe it's an essay, called 'When a Fulbright is not a Fulbright.'"

"I like her work. I would love to read that piece." Joyce sipped her champagne.

"Are you tired?" I asked my friends, hoping they wanted to get drunk on the excitement of us being in Europe together.

"Some, but we can always rest," Joyce announced.

"Now, Miss Joyce, you didn't tell me that girlfriend would be arriving wearing black leather pants," I said, pointing to Karla.

"You got that right," Karla said, blushing.

"You look great! How much weight did you lose?"

"About 40 pounds," Karla said proudly.

"Well, you go, girlfriend. Congratulations! That is no small feat. How did you lose it?" I asked.

"Jenny Craig. And it's easy. I didn't tell anyone in case it didn't work."

"It couldn't be that easy, or everyone would be doing it. I can't lose a kilo in this place," I said.

"A kilo. Look at Ms. International over here," Joyce said, nodding her head towards me.

"That would be Professor International to you," I sassed.

"Girlfriend is working it now," Joyce said.

"When did you decide to try dieting?" I asked Karla.

"One day, I saw myself in a photograph, and I didn't like what I saw."

"Alright. What did Russell say?" I wanted to know.

"Let's just say he noticed." Karla winked at us, grinning mischievously.

"Here's to 40 pounds and Russell," I toasted.

"Ethel, where can we go tomorrow?" Karla asked.

"Anywhere: Zürich, Switzerland, Strasbourg, France. They're all only about two to three hours away. We can get the early train in the morning and the last train back at midnight. A day is enough time to paint the globe, at least some of it. And just so you know, I hear that Tina Turner hangs out at the train station in Zürich," I said, loving the thought of showing my friends around, how I had become somewhat of an expert, at least a guide of sorts.

"That does it. We're going to Zürich." Joyce jumped and clapped.

"We have enough time to do both," I said, exciting them further.

"I can just see me when I get back home," Karla said. "I will be talking about my trip by saying, 'Oh, was it Switzerland? Or was it Germany? It could have been France since we did go to Strasbourg. What's a girl to do when her international memory fails her?'" Our laughter was as golden as the mango sun of Tübingen.

"Let's get organized," I said.

"Where should I put our bags?" Joyce asked, lugging their two heavy suitcases. I showed them their spaces, and we began unpacking. Immediately, we were into a routine, like sisters. I didn't feel like keeping my flat neat and organized was my job. It was our job, collectively. Joyce took the other bed in my room, and Karla stayed in the living room. Since I had a walk-in closet, I had allotted space for each of them. In Germany, you either had a walk-in closet or nothing. I was among the fortunate few.

As we skirted around my flat, sipping champagne, I played some Diana Ross and the Supremes. Joyce picked up one of the toothbrushes for a microphone and sang "Ain't No Mountain High Enough." Karla and I joined in. I used my brush for a mic, and Karla grabbed a bottle of lotion. Our next number was "I've Got Two Lovers."

"What do you think about Lauryn Hill?" I asked.

Karla picked up her lotion bottle and gave us a few lines of "Mr. Intentional."

"That's Silvia's favorite too," I said.

"She's your German teacher, right?" Joyce asked.

"Yes, and my friend. She's our age. I can't wait for you to meet her.

"Just think, when you go back home, you can say, 'Silvia, my German friend,'" Joyce said, giggling with glee. "Or 'the Englers, my German family.'"

"They really like you," Karla said.

"I know. It's great." I said.

"Were you afraid?" Joyce asked.

"You mean about coming here?"

"Yeah, especially by yourself and all. I don't know if I could've done it."

"I am afraid of everything, but I do it anyway," I said, thinking this was as good of a life motto as anything.

"You know how we do, girlfriend." Karla said.

"This language is so hard too. I don't know how you managed," Joyce said.

"That ain't half of it, but I've gained a lot from trying. It was miserable to learn, but I'm glad I tried so hard. It has allowed me to experience the country in a different way. Had my Fulbright only been for a semester, I wouldn't have gone through so much trouble learning the language, but I've been here a whole year," I said.

"Why don't you both apply for a Fulbright?" I continued.

"Just maybe I can with Bem being okay now," Karla said, referring to her son, who had just moved into a nice apartment with some friends.

"If I could get the husband away for long enough," Joyce said, thinking of Enoch.

"Bring him for a visit, let him meet some people!" I suggested. "He might like it here. Once you meet people, you see the place is just like any other place."

"Can you write German?" Karla asked.

"Very little. It's hard enough just trying to speak it. Speaking is more important, anyway. You have to make people understand you."

"More music?" Joyce walked over to the CD player with her hairbrush mic and played "Only Sisters Can Do That" by the Pointer Sisters, followed by "It Ain't A Man's World."

Joyce's lecture was scheduled for the second day after their arrival. Her presentation was excellent. Afterwards, she was able to relax without having to think about work anymore. It's hard to function in such a formal setting, with jetlag from an overnight flight. I must say, Professor Joyce Pettis' presentation was clear, insightful, and wonderful. Students were engaged and excited. They had already read *Brown Girl, Brownstones* by Paule Marshall, the focus of Joyce's paper.

After Joyce's presentation, I showed them around my office in Brecht Hall. They used my phone and computer to make contact with friends and family back home and catch up on necessary work. They loved the *Stadt*. After an early dinner at my favorite Italian restaurant, we walked up the hill and went to bed. Everyone was exhausted with exhilaration.

The next morning, our routine was as smooth as the cream yogurt I served for breakfast, along with the heavy jams and breads that were a must.

"And you wonder why I can't lose a kilo." I pointed to the spread on the table. Karla and Joyce had heard much about the bread, and they wanted to sample it. I had loaded up on all kinds of treats for them. I loved the brown crystallized sugar that popped when hot tea or coffee was poured on it. Joyce loved it too. I wished I had asked them to bring me some Equal, but I had forgotten. Well, it was too late now. I was almost through with my trip. Karla's success had motivated me; I would simply lose the 10 to 15 pounds when I got back home. It would help me reclaim my world.

We were ready to be out the door right on time to catch the eight o'clock train. I liked guests who said okay when you announced what time to be ready. My Seattle guest wanted to go to Baden Baden, but could only be ready by 11:00 a.m., which meant we had to take the local train that stopped in every village. She then complained that the train was too slow. We couldn't just sit in the non-smoking section, but we had to sit two seats away from the smoking section. Even though, she wasn't willing to run to catch the train.

Joyce was impressed that I understood the train station attendant, since he spoke so fast. I was impressed that she was impressed. I didn't bother to tell her that he says the same thing every time, or that I had heard it many, many times. I still felt some pressure being in charge of language. Karla knew some German, but barely enough for survival. No matter what, though, I knew neither would make fun of me like my Seattle guest, who spoke no languages, had done. Karla and Joyce would be helpful. That was also one of the joys of traveling with Rachel. Both of us were responsible and worked out problems together. Otherwise, I could travel alone.

On the train to Zürich, we agreed not to talk about *Paradise*, Toni Morrison's new novel. Joyce had not finished reading it, and she was working on a review of the book. Karla was reading Charles Johnson's new book about Martin Luther King. I had read it after a friend sent me an autographed copy. In spite of keeping my head and heart in Germany, I was hungry for anything to read in English. Anytime someone sent me a book, I sat down and read it immediately. It was like chocolate. I didn't tell them that I had a lot of trouble with *Paradise* and had finally turned to the reviews for help. Maybe Karla and I could talk about it when Joyce wasn't around. I was dying to chat about it with scholars.

"What do you think about *Honey Hush*?" Karla asked.

"It's beautiful, the anthology to die for. Anyone who's anybody is in it," I said.

"Daryl did a beautiful job, and she didn't bother me. You sent your work to her. I think I heard from her twice afterwards," Karla said.

"To tell you the truth, I wasn't sure she was going to use my work. Imagine how surprised I was when she used both pieces," I said.

"I know," Joyce said. "I wish I had submitted something."

"How did you find out that you were in it for sure?" Karla asked me.

"Well, the check for $75 and Opal called and said I was in it. And then I asked where I was. You know, next to what other authors?"

"That's just like a colored girl." Karla said.

"Yeah, once you're in, you want to know the company you keep."

"And?" Joyce asked impatiently.

"And what?"

"Who are you next to?"

"I'm between Zora Neale Hurston and Ann Petry."

"Is that good enough for the queen?" Joyce said.

"Yes ma'am."

"I love Nikki's introduction, and her piece is good too," Joyce said.

"I'm loving this book." Karla raised the Johnson book, stretched out on the seat. I hadn't liked it so much. Charles Johnson was a great short story writer. I wanted more of them. Karla liked him in the same way she liked John Edgar Wideman's writing.

"What is happening with Gayl Jones?" I asked.

"It's crazy, isn't it? Toni Morrison and Michael Harper are in charge of Gayl, I hear," Karla said. Joyce told us about a newspaper article she had read. Gayl's brother had said to the F.B.I., "You know we knew he's crazy, don't you?"

"Poor Gayl. Toni is right. Love is no better than the lover. Crazy lover means crazy love," I said.

"I still can't believe it. Sounds like one of the plotlines in her novels," Joyce said.

"There's so much mental illness among us," Karla said.

"How can there not be?" I asked.

"We're so used to just looking the other way," Karla said.

"How is it to live here?" Joyce asked.

"Okay."

"Really?" Joyce said, sensing that I wasn't telling everything.

"What about racism?" Karla asked.

"Well, most of the time, you forget it. Then, it happens, hitting you between your head and heart. But I do feel protected here."

"That's because you are," Joyce said.

"Is that feminism?" I asked.

"Being protected?" Karla asked.

"All of this is new to me," I admitted. "At home, I feel so alone most of the time. Although I know I am not, it stills just feels that way too much of the time."

"You mean at work? Or in your life?" Joyce asked.

"Both. I know work is not to be counted on for company."

"You're in a very nice setup here," Karla said.

"Thank you. I feel it, the support. It's how I dreamed collegiate life would be as a graduate student: sharing and exchanging ideas, not just living and breathing tenure talk or, worse, no talk at all."

"You don't have anything to worry about," Joyce said.

"Black women always have something to worry about, but with the book contract, I am not feeling the heat as much. It's all so hard," I said. The University of Missouri Press wasn't pressuring me about my manuscript, but I wanted to get it to them as soon as possible. I knew from other writers that the publishing world is as fickle as love, and this phase of the process can be fragile.

"What do you miss the most?" Karla asked.

"NPR."

"Is that all?" Joyce asked, surprised. "What about your house? Your place is so nice!"

"That's true, but if you live in a nice place, you don't miss what you left. Sometimes, something will remind me of my house. I miss going over to my friend Jane's house and picking flowers, or going shopping and giggling like girls. I miss my nice neighbors, Ann and Dick, who feed and love me. They nurture everyone in the community. Other than my encounter with Mr. and Mrs. Crazy Neighbor, I have caring neighbors. We look out for each other. "

"Do you think you could live here?" Joyce asked.

"Sometimes, but other times these Germans get on my nerves, girl. But I must say, I feel as close to Silvia, Ulli, and Rosemarie as I do to anyone."

"What about the language? Wouldn't you get tired of hearing it?" Joyce asked.

"I am sure I would, but if it's all you hear, I guess you get used to it. If I lived here, I would need more of a city than Tübingen." The seed and spirit of Berlin had been planted in me since the first time I visited the city. I will always return here, just as I will return to Paris and Venice again. If I lived in Germany, Berlin would be the place for me.

"What do you do when you're homesick?" Karla wanted to know.

"I walk in the *Stadt* and remind myself that the buildings are more than a thousand years old. I sit outside of a café and sip Prosecco. I breathe in."

Zürich is at the north end of Lake Zürich, with narrow streets and old-fashioned houses that contrast with its newer sections. The Limmat River divides the city into two parts, the Little City and the Great City. Eleven bridges cross the river to connect the two parts, the travel book told us.

My friends and I walked around in awe. First, we had tea at the *Bahnhof*, impressed that a train station could have so many designer names, first-rate restaurants, and glamour. No wonder Tina Turner hung out there. We felt like we were on Fifth Avenue in New York City.

"Can you believe we're in a train station?" Joyce raised her teacup, exposing her diamond wedding ring.

"It is grand," Karla agreed. "Ethel, you don't know this, but I collect cuckoo clocks. I have to add one from here to my collection."

"You should hear them all going off, Ethel," Joyce said, smiling at Karla.

"You're in the right place for cuckoos," I said. "That's one of the things the Swiss are known for."

"What else?" Karla asked.

"Swiss bank accounts," Joyce said, making us laugh.

"Guns, chocolate. Lately it's known for women voting against their own rights, against equality," I repeated a story from the news.

"Now that's progress we don't want," Joyce said.

"That's not all. Get this: they make some of the best wine in the world but don't feel a need to share it since they don't need the money," I said.

"What?" Joyce said.

"You heard me right," I confirmed.

We decided it wasn't our day to see Tina. Plus, we would have to come back to the train station on our way back to Tübingen. We continued strolling, laughing, and experiencing the old city part of Zürich.

"Were there ever any German colonies?" Karla asked.

"The way I understand it, the Germans got into the slave-holding game late," I said.

"But Germany is an old country," Joyce said, confused.

"Yeah, but it wasn't until the middle of the 19th century that it became the country that we recognize today. Before then, they had little regions with mad kings running around in the Black Forest or building castles," I said.

"That should say something positive about Germany," Joyce said.

"Well, it doesn't mean that they weren't investors in companies who owned slaves. They lost all of their colonies and slave interests after losing World War I," Karla said.

"It's not that they were so moral that they didn't have colonies," I said. "Take West Virginia, for example. Yeah, West Virginia broke away from Virginia over slavery, but it wasn't that they were so moral. They just had no use for slaves in the mountains," I continued.

"There's always use for slaves," Joyce said.

"But not in a big way, unless you have something to produce like in the South: crops of cotton, tobacco, and rice. But back to the Germans: they could make the Italians, Greeks, Turks, and the women do the unwanted work," I said as a light breeze picked up.

We continued walking, allowing the wind to guide us. The dimmed sky looked like dark gem hanging above us. The sun had faded beyond the river.

"Have you been here before?" Joyce asked.

"Yes, many times. It's a great day-trip."

"It's no wonder that the Europeans speak so many languages. They're all so close by," Joyce said.

"Yes, it's that and that the countries are manageable in size. None of the cities over here are as big as our biggest cities at home. They do not overwhelm me. I'm not even afraid," I said.

"I can I see that," Joyce said.

"We really do have too much violence at home," Karla said.

As the sky opened, we followed the sound of sweetness; music was coming from the Romanesque cathedral. A tiny old man was conducting a group of students in a violin lesson at the front of the church. We quietly poked around in the back of the church.

"One, two. One, two," said the tiny man, leading the students.

"We don't have to ask where he's from." Karla pointed to the flyers.

"Oh, my God." I put my hands over my mouth.

"What is it?" Joyce asked.

"That's Yehudi Menuhin." I pointed.

"It couldn't be," Joyce said.

"That's what this flyer says," Karla said, reading the flyer closely.

We took a seat in the back of the church in awe. Yehudi Menuhin is a prodigy violinist from New York City. By the time he was seven, he had appeared as a soloist with the San Francisco Orchestra, and at age ten, he played with the New York Symphony Orchestra. We read from the flyers and couldn't believe our luck. When Mr. Menuhin finished, we walked up to him and shook his hands. He autographed our flyers before he rushed off to his next appointment. We stayed and toured the beautiful church.

"Can you imagine living around buildings like this all the time?" Joyce asked.

"Yes, I can," I said. "I do." We laughed.

"Look." I pointed to the stained glass window. "That's a Marc Chagall."

"Are you sure?" Karla asked.

"Yes, I saw it with *Betrug*." I started to tear up, apologizing, "I'm sorry." All the memories about *Betrug* tumbled through my heart.

"Don't worry. You can cry all you want. I just love it that you don't use his name," Joyce said, comforting me.

"He isn't worth a name," I said, wiping my tears.

"Ethel, just think: when you write about this, he will be just one of your many lovers. Having lovers is part of the international experience," Karla said.

"You're right, girlfriend." I blew my nose. "I'm starved. Let's eat."

We dined in a too-expensive restaurant, eating luscious seafood with greens tossed in a raspberry dressing. That hole in my heart was being filled with love.

Joyce was impressed that I could handle the menu, but I told her they'd probably have one in English. Even if you could handle the menu as well as I had learned, translating is exhausting. However, my students had warned me that the English version of the menus was more expensive.

"What are folks saying about the new James Alan McPherson book?" I asked.

"Did you read it?" Karla asked.

"No, but I read the review. The one in The Washington Post was awful, but I sure do love his fiction." I continued, "He has a way of capturing specifics of the lives of Black folks, which we see less and less of in Black writing."

"He was plagued with mental illness." Karla looked in the distance.

"Really?"

"Yeah. Had a nervous breakup over a child custody case is what I heard."

"In the end, *Betrug* said that I was too serious." I couldn't contain myself any longer. I had to talk about him with my girlfriends.

"Why are we talking about *Betrug*?" Karla asked.

"Is he right?" I asked, looking from Karla to Joyce.

"Girl, don't think about that man. He has no idea what it takes to build a career in academia as a Black woman," Joyce said.

"Screw him," Karla said.

"I did." We laughed our way back into our moment.

After our extravagant lunch, we shopped in expensive shops. I bought a perfect rust-colored blouse that was marked down ninety percent, and Karla found a perfect cuckoo clock for her collection. Joyce and I marveled at it. Other than the glitch in the church, *Betrug* wasn't part of my space anymore. We didn't mention him again.

I had been saved by the support of friendship. Love is not about summing up what one had done, right or wrong. Love is more about accepting yourself and moving on, being proud that you survived with dignity. Suppose *Betrug* had waited to pull his little stunt after he had come to the States. It would've been far more costly. My girlfriends agreed I had dodged a bullet, which is what girlfriends always say when a relationship doesn't work out. I hadn't dodged the bullet at all. I had taken it in my heart.

On the midnight train to Tübingen, we settled into our seats, feeling like citizens of the world. My girlfriends and I couldn't have been happier.

"Can we really go to France tomorrow?" Karla asked.

"Yes, but I need to tell you that Bernd Engler has plans too. Tomorrow, we'll spend the day with him and his family hiking, and then Lucy will cook a feast."

"Marvelous! I'm hungry already." Joyce clapped her hands.

"They really treat guests great. I've never seen anything like it," I said.

"What are the students like?" Joyce asked.

"Interested. Respectful. Motivated. They really were excited about both your talks."

"What about teaching evaluations?" Karla asked.

"Well, they have them, but no one is required to submit them. In other words, they don't mean a thing."

"That would be nice. How are students supposed to know if you're an effective teacher?" Karla asked, shaking her head.

"If they learn anything," I said. We laughed.

"It's not important at home, unless they want to use it against you," Karla said.

"What burns me up is the way students don't give their professors enough credit on the evaluations. For example, take the question 'Does this professor come to class on time?' I always come to class on time. I am never late. If anything, I'm early. The problem is, when the students rate you as either excellent, good, or satisfactory, they mark 'good' rather than 'excellent.' Now, what's that about?" I asked.

"Racism," Karla announced. "We can never be excellent. It's a category saved for others."

"It's a stupid way to ask the question, anyway," Joyce said.

"That would never fly here. There's plenty of racism here. I'm just not the focus of it."

We were in a groove, laughing and comparing notes about our lives as Black American female professors, teaching at universities that our family members probably couldn't have attended forty years ago. The train wasn't crowded since it was midnight and not a holiday. I was exhausted. Only seeing Tina Turner could have made our day in Zürich more glorious.

A border patrol stood over me. I could have sworn it was the same one who had harassed Marcus and me last Christmas. I smelled his sweat and tobacco. My anger about patrols had been building since Austria and last Christmas. They were like the Klan hosing down citizens while their vicious German Shepherd dogs attacked in Montgomery and Birmingham, Alabama. He reached for my passport. I handed it over without looking at him, signifying that he didn't matter. I always felt some security in that I had a German work visa. He slowly gave it back to me. Both Karla and Joyce looked at their purses while holding their passports.

He then took Karla's passport and held it high, like he was having trouble reading it or checking to see if it was real. She had traveled to South Africa recently. We were international scholars and artists, and our traveling proved it. The border patrol tapped his fat sausage-looking fingers on the back of Karla's seat. We didn't look at him.

"What business do you have in this country?" The patrol asked without batting his eyes. Always the same nasty question, like he owned the country.

I spoke in the best German voice I had. "I am a guest of the German government. These important scholars are invited guests as well. Is there a problem?" I had not wanted to fight when Marcus was with me, but now I was with friends. It was our fight. The damned patrol should have been grateful that such distinguished guests were interested in visiting the country, which did not belong to him. He was only a citizen!

Rested and assured, we spent the next day with the Englers, traveling to Freiburg. There was no room in the van for mean border patrols as Bernd Engler's steady hands guided us toward our next experience.

Chapter 8

BLUE NOTES

*Voyagers discover that the world can never be larger
than the person that is in the world; but it is impossible
to foresee this, it is impossible to be warned.*

James Baldwin

We, Bernd Engler and I, drove Karla and Joyce to the Stuttgart Airport against the backdrop of a smoky sky. I felt like we were floating across the *autobahn*, sitting in the back with Joyce, missing them already. Their presence had given me the strength I needed to complete my journey. We were unusually quiet on this morning, knowing that parting was coming soon. That man I used to know, *Betrug*, had been put in his place —a footnote, a mere footnote, and after that, a mere memory – but my friends would always be my friends with long chapters in my narratives.

"Thanks for taking the boxes back." I tried to be light hearted. "Just mail it to my office."

"That's a good idea to give everyone something to take back," Joyce said.

"My friends should participate in all aspects of my international experience."

"Have you heard from many friends?" Joyce asked. Her eyes twinkled like honey, and her smile spread across her peach colored face, creating the most dramatic dimples.

"Those who want to travel to Germany," I answered.

"I heard that," Karla said in her soft-spoken but powerful voice.

"Too bad, most of my guests came before the warm weather. I needed coats and boots through April," I said.

"Now, if that was Miss Joyce, she'd just buy new clothes," Karla said.

"Not with German prices," I informed them.

"That's very true. Everything costs so much here," Bernd Engler confirmed. Eyes focused on the long gray highway.

"How do you manage?" Karla asked.

"Well, of course, we earn more money than Americans. I could never work for such low wages," Bernd Engler informed us, and we all agreed.

"Could you live in the States otherwise?" Karla asked.

"Not permanently." He spoke so matter-of-factly, "I would miss having a center of town. There is nothing more magnificent than having a place where everyone gathers."

"I am going to miss that the most." I felt tearful.

At the airport, I did cry. Everyone else did too, even Bernd Engler a little. Although I didn't see his tears, I felt them.

"What wonderful women," Bernd Engler said as we walked back to the car.

"The best." I tried to smile.

"Now, young lady, we have got to post your manuscript." He opened the car door for me.

I was happy to change the subject, too. If we had continued talking about Karla and Joyce, I would've wept. Talking about my work could get us all the way home, and I wouldn't have to keep crying about missing my friends.

"I couldn't have done it without your help, you know," I told Bernd. Even that kind of talk was making me weepy. I had to get a hold of myself.

"It's hard to do what you've done," Bernd Engler said.

"I can't believe the support from the entire staff," I continued. "Thank you again."

"It was our pleasure," he said, a smile curling the corners of his lips. He looked over his glasses at me, and I could see the urgency in his serious blue eyes when he told me, "It'll get harder."

"What? Getting the book published?" I asked.

"No, going back home," Bernd Engler said.

"It's complicated to have been here for a year. I wish I could stay, but not really." Our conversation had reminded me of Helmut, my old German boyfriend back in the United States. I could almost hear him saying those exact words when he left.

"And, of course, we'll miss you." Bernd Engler zoomed down the *autobahn*.

I knew they would miss me. Their last two Fulbright scholars hadn't worked out well. One had been an overly fussy male instructor from Duke or Vanderbilt; he had demanded an office with his own printer. Contrary to Germany's power in the world, while I was there, it seemed that they lagged behind American in technology with regard to office products. Their computers were old, big, and noisy. When I typed, whistles blew, which tickled the staff. They thought I was typing too fast. To print work, I emailed it to Tina, the assistant, and she'd print it and put the work in my mailbox. Bernd Engler, the chair, was the only person who had a printer in his office. I didn't think it was that big of a deal since Tina's office was only four doors down from me. Germans often didn't have answering machines in their homes either. Most people I knew in America had owned some sort of answering device since the early 1980s.

The other Fulbright scholar had been a woman who called them "a bunch of crazy Nazis." She stopped teaching her classes. When she did come to class, she would sometimes arrive in a costume to see what was being said about her. I heard this from some of my students. Other times, she shopped and traveled. The Fulbright Commission couldn't do anything about her behavior.

"I still think you should write a book about what not to do when publishing a book." Bernd Engler laughed.

"Very funny," I said, pretending to laugh. "So, for the rest of my natural life, you're going to hold it against me that my files were a mess."

"That, and the crazy woman you let in your class."

"Rosemarie has invited me to hike with her and Manfred around Lago Maggiore," I said, moving the subject away from my past failings.

"I just love it, Ethel. You always have some place to go. If I did not know any better, I would think you've lived here all of your life." He laughed for a long time, showing all of his teeth. "You're in for a real treat. I've been there many times. It is one of Lucy's favorite spots. Remember, we have lived around here a long time. When will you travel?"

"Next weekend, after the manuscript is in the mail." I raised my right hand and crossed my fingers.

"That's good timing. By the way, young lady, you did a terrific job with the guest lecture series, bringing so many dynamic scholars and lovely women to us."

"Thank you for calling me a young lady. Working on the lecture series, well, didn't feel like work at all. I enjoyed it." His erratic driving wasn't bothering me anymore. Maybe I had gotten used to it.

If I thought about all I had to do, I would feel overwhelmed. Getting my manuscript in the mail was the most important, but in the meantime, I still had to get ready for the US Embassy conference in Bonn. Everyone was calling it the 'last big bash' before moving to Berlin. I would be reading the last night of the conference with Paula Gunn Allen, a Native American writer I admired. I was thrilled. What a grand ending to a long and hard year!

During those hectic days, I missed Silvia. I couldn't imagine Germany without her. I even tried to keep up with my German lessons, but my heart wasn't in it. It was Silvia who had made learning a language interesting and fun. Everywhere I looked, I saw her. Walking around in our medieval town wasn't the same. When I heard laughter, a rare occurrence in Germany, I looked up and expected to see her, but she was in Oregon for a month, working. Her new position, the one for which we had written the proposal, had started already. Her father was ill. It must've been nerve-racking for her to leave a sick family member, especially an elderly parent, to travel to another country.

I hadn't realized how much I counted on Silvia. Getting a shawl made to wear to the Embassy reading was uneventful. Had Silvia been with me, we would have sipped coffee afterwards and talked about my German. I would've told her that I was nervous about my reading, and she would have calmed me, assuring me I was going to be a hit. She would have reminded me that I was becoming an important part of German history by reading in Bonn. Perhaps I would have practiced in front of her, an audience, until it would occur to me that I had been reading for audiences for more than 20 years.

GAWC invited me to one last excursion. I was sad since it was going to be our last time together, but I was happy to see them. Almost everything I did was for the last time, but there were a few people and places I could never say goodbye to forever. I knew it wouldn't be my last time seeing Silvia, Ulli, Rosemarie, or the Englers. Tübingen felt like home. I'll always return.

Seeing Ulli and Hiltrud would cheer me up. Ulli's father-in-law was terminally ill, and she had been caring for him. I was feeling lonely all over again. I was glad she could have a break too. Caring for a dying relative is challenging.

The Englers were sick with colds, and Horst Tonn was busy working on his lecture series. Rachael was traveling back and forth to the States, and I hadn't been able to track her down. I wondered if this was the beginning of my wanting to go home. I had lost three of my closest friends – not forever, but for the moment. I was feeling sorry for myself. Maybe this was what living abroad meant: fast friends, no real roots. That couldn't be true.

I loved spending time with GAWC. I was strictly a guest, and few things were better than being a guest in Germany. Our last trip was a tour of the Chancellor's Villa, which would be the governor's mansion in the States. After the tour, we would eat lunch there, in the huge and eloquent dining room. All ten of us were dressed in silk and linen suits with expensive shoes that hurt our feet. I wore a purple two-piece silk skirt and jacket and sported black leather shoes I had bought in Italy for my birthday. The moment we sat down, our shoes came off at the same time, and we laughed until our feet stopped hurting.

The military wives no longer annoyed me. They probably felt sorry for me after hearing about *Betrug*. Being in Stuttgart, I, of course, thought of him. He still crossed my mind now and then, but not nearly as much as when he first returned from South Africa. The night before, I had dreamed *Betrug* was standing in a fog, holding his hands out to me, but the closer I got to him, the less I could see him. He disappeared into the fog. What was he doing at this very moment? Would he live in South Africa with his new love? His love of place had always made me nervous. I don't understand the concept of loving land, other than owning your own home. Did he think of me? What had happened between us? Then, I remembered the last words he had shot through my heart: "I never want to see you again." After that lapse, he slipped out of my thoughts, and our small group moved forward with the afternoon.

Our program was hosted by the charming and funny Chief Deputy for the Chancellor and two tour guides. The Chief Deputy said that he had gone to the Universität Tübingen, but there hadn't been professors who looked like Professor Smith; otherwise, he would've made better grades and stayed at the Universität longer. Everyone clapped and laughed.

At the end of the luncheon, we were lined up to use the ladies room. Since there were no men present, I suggested we use the men's bathroom. A couple of women stood guard. The line was moving smoothly until our Chief Deputy appeared. The women who stood guard could only laugh. When some of us started out of the men's room, there stood the Chief Deputy. None of us could stop giggling. Ulli and I were in tears with laughter. The Chief Deputy chuckled too.

Classes were pretty much over. I was only meeting students to assist them with their final papers by reading their abstracts and drafts. Some students wanted to take me to a *Bier Garten* to show their appreciation and say goodbye. I wasn't in the mood for any more goodbyes. I was exhausted and tired of crying. Since I had sent boxes home with my guests, my office was emptying out. The end. It was over. I had almost completed the year. I would leave my note cards on the door. That would help. But help what? Was it for them to know that I had been here? Or for me to know that I had been here?

Not able to concentrate, I walked up the hill, home. My flat was looking empty and sad too. I sat down on the chunky blonde chair. All of the furniture was the same: steadfast and strong, like Germans. Why wasn't I ready to leave? I understood now what Anna had meant when she said she wanted to stay. Tübingen is so grand in its goldenness. It invites you to dream of staying, but as far as the Germans were concerned, you come and you leave. That was the deal. As long as the deal is upheld, all is well with the world.

I had already received an extension from the Fulbright Commission based on my need to complete grading papers. My new world wasn't feeling like home anymore. What had I not done? I never got to Prague. I had been too brokenhearted to accept Trish's invitation, since I was supposed to be there with *Betrug*. All of those ancient cities are too romantic. He had been a dream that turned into a nightmare, and like any natural disaster, it had ended. I had been lucky to survive.

Other than Prague, I had seen a lot of Europe; I had travelled through most of Germany, Austria and Switzerland. I had traveled to Paris to spend a long weekend with my friend Anne Warner and her daughters. Donna Blagg and

I had spent some lovely holidays together in the Alsace, Munich, and Venice. I felt the tiredness of my travels. What would I find at home? I needed rest. After rest, could I endure the dreadful bleakness of living alone in West Virginia? What doors would my Fulbright open for me back home? Would my colleagues treat me with respect? In spite of my hopeful future, I still felt numb.

Early the next morning, I walked down the hill to the *Holzmarkt*. The Greek ladies were shocked to see me before 8:00 am. I couldn't bear to tell them that I would be leaving soon. This is what I would miss most about living in a medieval town: walking down lanes, looking up and being surprised. That morning, I spent hours examining and enjoying old tavern signs. It was something Silvia and I had done many times. Flowers of festive colors flourished from almost all balconies and windows. Artistic figures and graceful fountains embellished squares and small gardens outside of homes. Small bridges and alleys, passageways and arcades are shortcuts into the center of Tübingen, its heart and soul. How could I leave this place? Tübingen had held me captive in its beauty, awakening my mind in ways I couldn't have imagined one year ago. I was in love, and it felt good to be able to love again.

Two days later, I sipped Prosecco in my office with Bernd Engler, Horst Tonn, Hartmut Grandel, and Oliver Scheiding. Our toasts blessed my manuscript's journey to the publisher, assuring its safe arrival. We raised our glasses with the hope

that the readers would have vision, that they would understand the importance of my work.

"To the manuscript!" Bernd Engler raised his glass.

"To all of you." I raised my glass. "I couldn't have got this
done without your help. I will always be grateful."

"We know that," Horst Tonn said.

"To the future! May we all have grand ones," I proclaimed.

"*Prost*," they all said, as our glasses sang out loud.

Rosemarie and Manfred met me at the train station in
lovely Locarno, Switzerland. Having someone to meet you
at a train station is wonderful, but having friends meet you
is most wonderful. In spite of the overnight train, trip I felt
rested and excited. I was thankful that the manuscript was
in the mail. Maybe I could even relax. I had no trouble with
the mean border patrols this time. Rosemarie had sent me
an email at the last minute to remind me that I was coming
to Locarno, not Lugano. I was glad; I had mixed up the two.
My recurring nightmare almost came true.

Locarno is the Italian-speaking Switzerland, located on
the northern tip of Lago Maggiore in the southern Swiss can-
ton of Ticino. Marino Vigano, an Italian historian, speculated
that Locarno's castle may have been designed by Leon-
ardo da Vinci, according to the tour guide. As Rosemarie,
Mandred, and I strolled through the old town, I felt like I was
having an Italian holiday. Patrician houses with concealed
balconies bear witness to the supremacy of the once
wealthy trading metropolis. Galleries, shops, and cafés line
the lanes of the city, which also claims the mildest climate

in Switzerland. Locarno's landmark is the pilgrimage church of Madonna del Sasso, a place of prayer with extraordinary views of the lake and mountains.

The *Astrovia Locarno* is a 1:1,000,000,000 scale model of the Solar System. The sun can be found at the end of *Via Gioacchino Respini* where the cycle path runs alongside the river. Pluto, the final planet in the model, can be found six kilometers away from this starting point in the village of Tegan. If you want to see all the planets, it is preferable to cycle rather than walk; those who walk rarely go farther than Saturn, according to the guidebook.

Rosemarie has fond memories of visiting Locarno when she was a child. Her adopted aunt is buried there. The woman was engaged to Rosemarie's uncle, but when he did not return from the War, his family adopted her.

We all lived in an indoor camp-like setting. Rosemarie and Manfred shared a room, and I had a room of my own. It was quite comfortable, and I liked the comfort of their routines. Rosemarie eats one slice of cake or pie a day – never more, never less. It reminded me of Silvia's chocolates in her purse. Other than Rosemarie's love and passion for art, languages, and scholarship, she loves the outdoors.

The view of Lago Maggiore took my breath away. I wish I'd brought binoculars. Two Italian regions share the lake: the eastern shore is nestled in Lombardia, and the western side of the lakes is the northeastern corner of Piemonte. The Baroque '*Madonna della Guardia*' sits next to a medieval watchtower with spectacular views of the Ossola Valley and the *Corni di Nibbio* peaks. I was in heaven!

On our first full day, we got in three and a half hours of hiking before a continuous and heavy downpour started. Indoors, Rosemarie and I were happy to read. Manfred was a bit more anxious. He's a tall and gentle man, one of the first men to take a maternity leave. He'd left his position as a detective to care for his three daughters after his wife, Rosemarie's best friend, passed away. Manfred's English was better than my German, but he still struggled. I was more sympathetic to his English woes than Rosemarie, but, then again, I didn't live with him. I was a good English teacher to Manfred, and I was learning German from him. I learned something about the German language with everyone I encountered.

By evening, the rain had stopped and the sky cleared. We walked into the village via the grottos and dined at an Italian restaurant that had delicious food and a fine ambience.

The next day, we hiked most of the time. Had I been with my Aussie friends, we would have shopped, but my German friends don't shop that much. Locarno was what I needed: relaxation, exercise, and time away. Tübingen had begun to close in on me; I had so much to do once I got back, but thinking about it overwhelmed me. With Rosemarie and Manfred, I didn't have to make any decisions other than what I wanted to eat or which direction to walk.

At the end of my long weekend in paradise, Rosemarie, Manfred, and I took the train back together from Stuffgart. They would travel to Frankfurt, while I would return to Tübingen. I was ready to face my remaining days.

One of my favorite train rides is along the Rhine River. It's the route to Bonn and Cologne. The train ride absorbed my worries. I eased my thoughts toward my upcoming conference, "Across Borders." I was going to talk about the psychological borders in the States, the borders left by slavery. I had lived in the texts of the slave narratives. Regardless of the audience, talking about slavery is tricky, just in different ways. My panel included one other American and a Canadian historian. I was also scheduled to give a talk about my book-in-progress that I had just mailed to the publisher. The book became *From Whence Cometh My Help: The African American Community at Hollins College*. And finally, there would be the reading for the last dinner. I felt exhausted just thinking about the tight schedule, but it was the distraction I needed.

The Romans constructed a bridge across the Rhine close to a place called "Bonna" around 10 BC. The fort became a town, which remained after the Romans left. Between the 11th and 13th centuries, the Romanesque style Münster was built. Bonn became the capital of the principality of Cologne in 1597. After that, the town gained more influence and grew considerably, stated the guidebook.

After Germany reunification, Berlin became the nominal capital of Germany again, which was decided by parliament on June 20, 1991, after a heated debate, of course. While the government and parliament moved, some of the ministries largely remained in Bonn, with only the top officials in Berlin. There was no plan to move these departments, and Bonn has remained a second, unofficial capital with the new title of *Bundesstadt*, Federal City. Due to the necessary construction work, the move wasn't completed until 1999.

I arrived early, June. The summer had turned cold and wet. After checking into the hotel, I shopped for a sweater or a jacket. Bonn is beautiful and easy to get around. I toured the Beethoven House Museum. Before I went back to the hotel, I visited the Münster. While I was in Europe, I always visited cathedrals. I would light candles and pray for world peace, ask for blessings for everyone in need. That's precisely what I did in Bonn on that chilly June afternoon.

When I got back to the hotel, other conference participants had started to arrive. My first thought was, there are too many Americans. I had forgotten how uncomfortable I felt around them, as they conversed about their wealth and privilege. I had to remember that my truth wasn't their truth. Blacks and whites have different reference points in America, different truths. It didn't matter if we grew up in the same place, attended the same schools, or worked at the same jobs. Our worlds didn't often meet until adulthood, if then. I believed that was why I was invited to Germany, to give my perspective.

"We would like to talk more about contemporary history," the other American panelist said. I wanted to ask him who made him king of my presentation, but I didn't want the talk to turn ugly.

"Slavery is part of America's contemporary history. We only have contemporary history," I kept a steady voice. I was not going to get defensive. Finally, the panel discussion ended. I knew that the rest of the program would be better. I would be responsible for only myself and my work, the beauty of not being on a panel.

After the session ended, many of the Germans came up to me and thanked me for talking about our history in an honest manner. Germans seemed more willing to talk about their scars of the Holocaust. By that time, I was too tired to care about the panel. Done for the day, I went to my room and took a nap. Rain poured liked daggers falling from the sky.

The next day, the brightness of an early summer morning sun guided us to an open market. Bonn is famous for its open markets. I felt rested and assured. Paula Gunn Allen was ill and needed to change times with someone. I was happy to oblige. By evening, she was feeling better, and we ate dinner together. We got along well, and she even noted my Native American cheekbones. I told her my great-grandmother was half Cherokee. She wasn't surprised.

Later, on her panel, a member of the audience asked Paula about relations between Native Americans and African Americans. Her answer shocked and saddened me. "We don't trust them," she answered. How could she say such a thing? More than 40% of African Americans were mixed with Native Americans. I sat stunned. This conference had turned into a horror show for me. I wish I had stayed at home.

Finally, the last night arrived. With the many visiting dignitaries, the lecture halls were decked out for such a historic event. The attendees were dressed up as well. My reading was a hit! I was thrilled, and even more so to leave the next morning.

Three days later, I received a telephone call from Klaus. Silvia's father was dying. She was coming in on an emergency flight. How awful. Poor Silvia must have been terrified. I asked Klaus if there was anything I could do. He said no, but thanked me.

He was right. There was very little anyone could do. Silvia arrived two days before her father died. I didn't call her. She had enough to worry about. Her mother was her major concern, but first she had to bury her father.

In the meantime, Ulli's father-in-law had also died. I felt darkness all around. I wrote Silvia and Ulli letters. That seemed to be so little, but it was all that I could do.

My sister telephoned to tell me two of my high school classmates, with whom I had been close, had also died. One from a massive heart attack, and the other from AIDS. Both were under 45. My head was spinning with the sadness of death. I was glad that Anna was coming in a few days. I hoped she could help me get through these dark moments of desolation. I was worried that I would disappoint her with all of my woes. She was excited to be coming back, and I was relieved to be leaving.

I sat in my office, feeling ready to cry, but I needed to feel useful. There was so much to do. I hadn't been checking my email on a regular basis. Cleaning out my email messages, I found a note from my renters. Brandon, my 17-year-old cat, was sick. His kidneys were failing. Immediately, I telephoned my vet, who told me that Brandon needed to be put to sleep. I emailed my renters and gave them the information, asking them to bury him under the lilacs in my backyard. I locked my office door, put my head on my desk, and wept.

My emotional exhaustion continued. When Anna arrived from the States, I was so happy to be saying hello to someone rather than goodbye. Anna's German is good. She had made her way from Stuttgart to Tübingen with no problems. She'd even rented a car. I was impressed; the idea had never occurred to me. I felt good that I could get around via trains, buses, taxis, etc.

There was so much to talk about, which took my thoughts away from the looming end of the year. I was even happy to hear about my department at WVU, as Anna and I walked around under the summer sun of Tübingen. Anna showed me some of her favorite places. I felt stronger. She had helped with the packing and organizing the end of my trip. I couldn't lug all of my stuff with me to Stuttgart and then to Greece, so I sent some boxes to Rosemarie. She and Manfred were going to meet me at the airport in Frankfurt when I left for home. Finally, I had help. Though I wasn't used to it, I was happy to have someone to count on.

I hadn't realized how lonely I was. Plus, Anna's German was a wonderful relief. Two days wasn't enough. All, too soon, Anna returned to Stuttgart for her conference. We planned to reunite there on my way to Greece, if Silvia decided to go. Once again, I was saying goodbye, even though it was only temporary.

The next day, glorious and golden Tübingen turned gloomy. In drizzling rain, I went to the cinema. In the Sates, I went all the time alone. It never bothered me. I saw *Lolita* with Jeremy Irons. I figured I couldn't go wrong, being that I already knew the text. In Tübingen, all of the films were in German with no subtitles. The only film I saw in English was *The Full Monty*, but the Liverpool accents were so thick that I would've understood it better had it been in German.

I went to the cinema a lot in Germany with Silvia and Klaus, and with Horst Tonn. I had seen: *One Fine Day, Foxy Brown, The Big Lebowski, The Better It Gets,* and many documentaries. Though it was in German, I understood the plotlines fairly well. Still, I planned to watch the films again once I was home to see just how much I missed.

Jeremy Irons is one of my favorite actors, and he was terrific in the *Lolita*. When the film ended, I walked outside. The rain was gone, and the sun was shining again. I sat outside in the *Holtzmarkt* and sipped Prosecco, knowing that I would be okay. Across the street stood the *Heckenbauer* booksellers, where Herman Hesse had been an apprentice. I enjoyed a view of the church's nuptial, gate, and stairway. I always sat in the same seat, across from the bookstore. I had learned everything that surrounded it.

In 1983, a slab was placed there to commemorate the Jews of Tübingen who had been deported and killed. A fountain of St. George made of stone had been erected in 1976. Other than serving as a market site, the *Holtzmarkt* is a place for musicians to play. No music was playing that day, but my seat gave me an excellent view of the Lower City, the New Street, and the Pfleghof und Neckargasse.

The next day, I heard from an exhausted and sad Silvia. She wanted to get together. I heard all of the details of her harrowing trip; she had arrived in time to say goodbye to her father. She wasn't sure if we would go to Greece or not. I told her not to worry. I could live without another trip. Even though I had already purchased my ticket, I was sure that I could return it. Germans were good about allowing you to change tickets without such a fuss or penalty. I needed to go to the travel agency to work out the details for my return and figure out how to meet Marcus in Edinburgh. I had to tell Marcus about Brandon too. Was there anything that I didn't have to do?

Silvia, Klaus, and I met for premiere party for the showing of a film called *Blue Note*, a great venue for our first meeting. Had we met in a more private setting, I might have fallen apart. I wanted to be strong for Silvia, who looked thin and worried. My breakdown could wait until I got home.

"Oh, Ethel, it has been so difficult," Silvia said as we embraced.

"I'm sure, but you're not alone."

"I know, Ethel. Thank you."

We sat in the old theatre, hoping the gala event would replace our pain and panic. Blue Note is a jazz record label, established in 1939 by Alfred Lions and Francis Wolff. Its name comes from the characteristic "blue notes" of jazz and the blues. Blue Note is often associated with the "hard bop" style of jazz: mixing bebop with other forms of music like soul, blues, rhythm and blues, and gospel. Horace Silver, Jimmy Smith, Freddie Hubbard, Lee Morgan and Art Blakely were among the label's leading artists, but almost all of the important musicians in post-war jazz recorded for Blue Note on occasions.

Alfred Lion is a German who first heard jazz as a young boy in Berlin. In 1939, two years after moving to New York, he recorded Albert Ammons and Meade Lux Lewis in a one-day session in a rented studio. At first, the label consisted of Lion and Max Margulis, a communist writer who funded the project. The label's first releases were traditional hot jazz and boogie-woogie. Its first hit performance was "Summertime" by Sidney Bechet. The presenter told us musicians were given alcoholic refreshments, and they recorded in the early hours of the morning after their evening's work in clubs and bars. The label soon became known for treating musicians well, especially African Americans who couldn't get their music produced in their own country.

The director of the film was a Tübingen graduate. At the end of the documentary, we could ask questions in English. Since several Americans and Germans were interviewed, the documentary was in both German and English.

Silvia, Klaus, and I were caught up in the dazzling act of jazz improvisation. Just like our lives, the music moved us in and out of the past, present, and future. The music carried us back to slavery, the Holocaust, and the Civil Rights Movement. And it carried us forward to the hope of a healing future for a complex humanity. I discovered that I was aware through the music of Art Blakely, Ron Carter,

John Coltrane, Miles Davis, Herbie Hancock, Joe Hender-
son, Bobby Hutchinson, Thelonious Monk, Sonny Rollins, and
Stanley Turrentine, and all of the other greats. I had found
my path through the map of my soul, and most importantly,
I had learned to follow it. I found my way out of sadness and
loneliness into a new dream.

Chapter 9

THE END OF THE DREAM

*The adventure is over. Everything gets over, and nothing
is ever enough. Except the part you carry with you.*

E.L. Kongsburg

My German friends and I have shared many marvelous moments together since I left Germany. We have found ways to stay close. Silvia, Ulli, and Rosemarie have visited me here in West Virginia. I have met them in Italy, New York City, and Maine. Since I left, I have traveled to Germany a few times too. Silvia is the Resident Director of OUS International Programs in Germany for the Universität Tübingen, which means she travels to Oregon at least once a year. Rosemarie has a house in Maine, where her sister lives. I've visited her several times there.

In 2009, Silvia invited some friends from Hamburg to join us in NYC. My son lived in the area, and he spent time showing us around. They wanted to stay at a Bed & Breakfast. I didn't, but I wasn't going to make a fuss. I am not fond of the idea of servants or anything that represents plantation life. I preferred a hotel like the Marriot, etc. I didn't feel like explaining this to Silvia, who found a small B&B on the Upper East Side.

Silvia made the arrangements and submitted my name as part of the group of five individuals. She told me to be prepared to pay cash for my portion of the invoice, which seemed curious, but I came prepared. Silvia also told me the proprietor of the B&B was holding her credit card information. I could arrive anytime that day, but I was told not to pay until everyone had arrived.

On the day of our arrival, I telephoned the B&B to see if it was okay for me to come a couple of hours earlier than my friends, since they were still in-flight. I wanted to buy flowers for the apartment to welcome them to America. The person I spoke to confirmed that I was part of the group. She said, "That would be lovely. We'll see you soon."

Yet, when I arrived, I was not allowed in the apartment. I was told that they didn't give the key to "just anyone." I tried to explain to the woman that I had just spoken to her on the phone; I recognized her voice. It seemed useless. She asked for a credit card and a passport. I told her that I knew they were holding Silvia's credit card information, and, as a sixth generation American citizen, I was not in the habit of carrying my passport with me in my own country. I complied as well as I could, offering my driver's license and university identification, but I still was not allowed in the apartment. I gave up, and I resigned myself to just wait for my friends. I thought I'd go out for a cup of coffee, but I wasn't even allowed to leave my luggage without paying a $50 fee. I refused. I was left sitting in the vestibule on a small, hard chair for nearly three hours. No one spoke to me the entire time. In fact, they closed the door so they wouldn't have to see me. I was shocked; we were paying over $600 a day, and this was how I was being treated.

I didn't know what to do. I telephoned Silvia, but she was still in flight. As soon as her plane landed, she called me back. I explained what had happened. In disbelief, she called the B&B and insisted that they allow me into the apartment. She was told they would rather wait until she arrived.

When my friends finally arrived, the proprietor ignored me and dealt with them. I was the only person who had enough cash for my portion. Others had to wait until the next day since they were just arriving. The proprietor had no trouble with that. We were all upset, but didn't have much of a choice but to stay. We were exhausted, and I didn't want our short time together further ruined. Fortunately, we didn't see any staff for the rest of our time there.

Back home, I wrote a letter to the owners, assuming they would want to know what had happened to me. All I wanted was a genuine apology. A few days later, I received an unsigned letter on plain white paper from the proprietors, telling me that what I claimed couldn't have possibly happened.

Frustrated, I wrote a negative review of the B&B on a travel website, simply stating what had happened to me. A few weeks later, I received a telephone call from the Dean at my University. He and the President of the University had received a long, ranting letter from the proprietors of the B&B. The Dean told me not to write personal letters on University stationery; I hadn't thought it would be a problem when I wrote to the B&B owners. He was keeping my letter on file, to prove that he had given me such instructions. I was in a state of shock. I didn't have the energy to get into any kind of exchange with him. I didn't bother to explain my reasoning. I had been working on my manuscript, and I needed my German colleagues to help me with the German language in the book. I had every right to use a University letterhead; much of the trip was about my work.

I read the letter from the B&B, which began by buttering up the Dean, telling him what a good family man he was. The letter went on:

"Recently, we received a letter from Ms. Ethel Morgan Smith, Associate Professor at your English Department. The letter, written on your letterhead, has troubled us tremendously. Ms. Smith made serious accusations towards one of my staff members. If true, the actions would constitute the firing of the employee. Clearly, our accounts of the incident are quite different than those described by Ms. Smith. We understand that individuals occasionally exaggerate and twist facts to align with her personal agendas. Ms. Smith may feel that it was rude for us to refuse her entry into her room before receiving payment, but for her to interpret our universally applied business policy as an act of racism is quite a leap. At best, Ms. Smith's interpretation of our actions was misguided. It may be attributed to the fact that individuals often are predisposed to interpret situations consistent with their beliefs, whether those beliefs are justified in that situation or not. At worst, she is a pariah preying on hard-working individuals with false race card motivations.

Unfortunately, by using University letterhead, she has involved your school in this matter. What makes Ms. Smith's allegations even more surprising is that the staff member in question is an upstanding individual. She came to us extremely well regarded by prior employers. She is a graduate of one of the most rigorous Ivy League academic programs in the country. She holds a degree in theological studies and has volunteered extensively in the developing world.

Our only guess as to how Ms. Smith could even remotely misread racial implications into our assistant's interaction is that she was relatively new to her position. Perhaps she was unsure of how to respond to Ms. Smith's aggressiveness. We can imagine the feigned indignity Ms. Smith demonstrated when learning that she would need to pay for her stay before receiving room keys, just like other guests. The awkwardness Ms. Smith created by insisting on waiting in the lobby tor nearly three hours, instead of taking a brief walk, probably compounded our assistant's discomfort.

Your University is a fine institution that is now being dragged into an ugly incident due to Ms. Smith's actions. She must be held accountable. We would like her to write an apology to us on the same University letterhead, rescind her review on TripAdvisor.com, and send letters of retractions to all other entities she has contacted.

We are planning to enter litigation over Ms. Smith's slanderous remarks. The longer this slander remains public, the larger the potential recourse to Ms. Smith and your University. In addition to damages, we will be seeking supervisory sanctions by the University in regard to Ms. Smith's recklessness and disregard for an upstanding member of the New York City business community. Perhaps Ms. Smith takes the chair in our lobby for the back seat of a bus in 1962 Montgomery, AL, but to claim racism here is disrespectful to all those who have not been allowed into hotels or country clubs because of their face. While her behavior is ugly, it is her right, but she crossed the line is by posting her delusion on one of the most well-known hotel websites.

Our next letter will be to the appropriate accrediting bodies in respect to one of their members and faculty. We will give you the courtesy of a response before we take this step. We thought you should know that a member of your faculty is demonstrating such fractious behavior."

I am a friendly international scholar and writer. I grew up in rural Alabama and spent much of my adult life in Atlanta, Georgia. I have travelled and lived in Europe, Australia, Mexico, and New Zealand. Though I have traversed much of the world, I have never encountered such treatment. Of course, I have encountered racism before; I live in West Virginia and teach at a University with less than 5% African American students. On any given day, I can be insulted by a cashier, a waiter, a student, or even a colleague, but nothing comes close to this unbelievable insult.

I read the letter from the B&B more than ten times. Each time, I was more stunned than the time before. After the fifth read, my literary instincts kicked in. I was reminded of poet

Phyllis Wheatley, who had to go before the August group to prove that she was the author of her first book of poems. I was reminded of Jamie Crawford, the protagonist in *Their Eyes Were Watching God*, who had to go before the court to defend herself. Finally, I was reminded of the Anita Hill and Clearance Thomas hearings. I was in good company.

No one supported me. My Dean had hired me and knew me well, but the only support I got was a letter in my file, telling me not to write personal letters on University letterhead.

At no time was the proprietor in any danger of not being paid. After all, they were holding my Silvia's credit card information. They simply did not want me there, and I did not want to be there. Did they think my German friends wouldn't be affected by their behavior? They would never set foot in such a place again.

Was this the new post-racial era? We, Black Americans, tell ourselves that we are used to systematic racism, but even if we are, it hurts and wears on our health and our souls. Is this the future of race relations in America? My German friends could not understand why my home had treated me so cruelly, nor could I.

I had to remind myself who I was by rediscovering that map to my soul. I had to remember the ancestors and what they had endured. Of course, the racism at the B&B wasn't anything new to Black folks in America, but it felt like salt had been poured on an old wound, one that had never healed. I knew the ancestors were cheering me on, especially my mother and grandmother.

Epilogue

"MY GERMAN AFRICAN AMERICAN CIRCLES" BY ROSEMARIE ABENDROTH

In 1997 I got to know Ethel Morgan Smith; we became friends first and then close friends, we laugh about the same things and we get upset about the same things. We share political opinions; sometimes we disagree. We also compare our different family and "men" stories. I remember hiking together around Tübingen along lakes and through woods, fields, and vineyards without meeting a lot of other people. Ethel asked me whether it was safe to hike alone; she had a strange feeling. When she was young she was not supposed to go away farther from her house because of safety reasons. Ethel grew up in a small town in Alabama. The discrimination in the society in Alabama of the time and the Civil Rights Movement had a significant impact on her childhood and youth. She was 11 years old when the bombs exploded in the 16th Street Baptist Church in Birmingham that took the lives of four little girls attending Sunday school. All Black families had to limit the lives of their children to keep them away from areas where they might face danger.

Even though I am almost a decade older than Ethel, we have experienced some of the important political incidents together in our adult life, *diesseits und jenseits des großen Teichs*/on this side and the other side of the big pond, as we confer to jokingly in German. I was thrilled to read Ethel's *Reflection of the Other: Being Black in Germany*, an outside view on Germany by an African American friend. Belonging to that part of the post-war German generation we never identified so much as German; European is what we rather consider ourselves. We go along with a critical view on Germany. For the following generations the recent past was not as determining. My children belong to the new generation of Germans who take a certain pride in being German and view themselves as equals in the global community.

Reading *Reflections* I found myself asking and comparing, to my own surprise, is that really us? Usually, I do not regard myself as part of the *us*. But still I have to remind myself constantly I am but one German whom Ethel encountered. It is not so much the saddening and frightening incidents at the station in Rostock or at the border to Switzerland that I disagree with. I have personally witnessed with Ethel the haughty comportment of the border control. We were on our way to a hiking tour at the Lago Maggiore. When the train passed into Switzerland the border police checked our passports. We were about five people in the compartment and the same moment the police looked at the passports they gave them back to us, except for Ethel's passport. They checked her passport, in a smug way leafed through the document, looked through some other papers until I could not stand it anymore and asked them what the matter was. Reluctantly, they gave back Ethel's passport without explanation.

As sad as it is I know these things might happen. They are the small things that leave a big question mark for me. We, the post-war generation wanted to be completely different from our parents. We rejected the so-called *Preußischen Tugenden*/the Prussian Virtues like order, punctuality and effectiveness. These were obviously some of the traits that led to the authoritarian behaviour of Germans in the first half of the century. Ethel's perspective on Germans still today leads along this Prussian path. When I read her commentary on the promptness of the German train system I had to laugh out loud. Today, only ten years later, people complain constantly that it is almost the norm that trains are not on time, and strikes of the engine drivers are disturbing schedules.

I was really disappointed learning that one of Ethel's students in Tübingen thought it was necessary to experience the phenomenon of 'passing.' I have worked for 20 years at an elementary school where we had up to 60 % Turkish children in class along with children from other nations. There were joy and problems with all children alike. The stories we read came from all parts of the world, most of our parents committed their time preparing school and class festivities and theatre plays. Children in class learned from invited parents about Islamic holydays and we celebrated in a cultural, not religious way, Christmas together. Turkish parents baked with German parents German Christmas cookies and German parents learned from Turkish parents how to bake the cheese filled pasta breads. All children were competing in writing poems and playing soccer. There were no losers; and the very successful came from a diverse background. We all worked hard, parents and teachers alike to overcome obstacles that were certainly there. In elementary school there is still a great impetus to work for a structure that allows every child to be part of the community.

I know that problems grow when students continue their education, and if parents and young people face economic difficult times even unemployment. But reading about Ethel's Turkish student, that she felt compelled to 'pass' in class made me especially sad, questioning myself about the result of our teaching.

Ethel has not written a statistical research on Germany, but her personal experience as an African American professor living and teaching in Germany for a year. And what is more important her *Reflections* are not so much about Germany, but as a German reader, I am inclined to accept her observations. It is more about Ethel's life, her personality, and what the German year meant for herself, her love, her career, her friends, and her country. With Ethel's humorous manner I certainly found great delight in reading the *Reflections*. It gave me the chance to deepen my relationship with Ethel and to reconsider my own self-image.

I was two years old in April 1945 towards the end World War II. I remember sitting on a handcart that my mother was pulling back into the small town, half burnt down. This provincial town of Calau of about 8,000 inhabitants is located

80 km south of Berlin. My mother was literally and figuratively strong as a horse according to a picture an aunt conveyed to me; she wore a broad leather belt around her shoulder and breast walking back into her hometown. She led on one hand my seven-year-old sister, my five- year-old brother, on the other hand my 80-year-old weak grandmother, and me, the two-year-old, sat on top of a mattress on the handcart.

The important Nazis had already left town with their belongings before the Russians arrived, not without giving orders to the staunch believers to defend the town to the last drop of blood. Even though the population did not go along with that, there were some Nazi-idiots who tried to defend on the cost of their own population. That is why the Russians set fire to the town before entering and people had to leave the town for a few days.

My mother found her three-family house fortunately not burnt down, but full of refugees of the Eastern parts of Germany, who needed a roof over their heads, on their trail towards the West; some stayed there, some continued westwards. The stream of refugees was a common picture in town from autumn 1944 on. Generally the people of the town tried to help since some of the refugees had already been trailing westwards for weeks 300 km and more.

One of the coldest winters followed. The Soviet soldiers and the East German population suffered of hunger and cold since they did not have enough food, wood or coal. On the same handcart my mother brought only nine months later the casket with her dead mother to the cemetery, because my grandmother Agnes starved to death rather than not share her spare rations of food with her grandchildren. Accompanied only by my sister and aunt my mother found the cemetery earth too frozen to bury my grandmother. They had to wait two weeks to lay her into the burial ground. I write this not to complain about the German fate after the War, but to admire the strength of my mother to fight for the survival of her children and her own mother.

I studied history in high school and at the Johann Wolfgang Goethe- *Universität* in Frankfurt a. Main. When I was a teenager and as an adult, I tried to find out what was going on in my own family history in Nazi-time. So I am aware of the horrible uniqueness of German history in that time, incomparable in its horror. As many Germans of my generation I had to deal with the terror of our parents-and grandparents' generation.

From 1990 through 1993, I did additional studies in American and English culture and literature and educational science at the *Universität* Frankfurt and at the University of Massachusetts in Amherst. Among others I concentrated on African American, Caribbean and Nigerian history, literature, and global educational transfer-systems. I widened my intellectual horizon concerning other histories and cultures, and at the same time I was always thrown back into German history.

As the population in the Eastern Zone suffered from hunger and cold in 1946 CARE-Parcels arrived pretty soon from generous Americans in the Western Zones of occupied Germany.

American and British soldiers had their own facilities and did not have to participate in the German food and heating system, but the Russian Army was forced to. Friends who had grown up in the American Zone told me it was a feast for them as children to unwrap the chocolate, and how their mouths watered when their mothers prepared hot cocoa for them, maybe one time every two months from water or powdered milk.

Around the same time, African American soldiers in Paris relished the freedom to get around without reading at the entrance of bars, jazz-clubs and shops, the embarrassing "Only for Whites." African American soldiers were not yet integrated, and the American Military government under General Eisenhower tried to tell the French government to refuse admission to American Black soldiers. The gist of what the French under General De Gaulle proudly answered was, "In our country everyone has the right to go wherever they want to." General Eisenhower already had announced a corresponding plan to make out of France an American military zone with an American Military Governor. Imagine General Eisenhower Military *Gouverneur de France*. From 1953 on the Americans chose the Spanish Fascist General Franco to sign a treaty for military bases in Spain. General Franco, who only eight years before was Hitler's ally. This "General Franco"-American friendship lasted until 1975 when Franco died. Then the Spanish people voted for democracy and got rid of their dictatorship themselves. They even succeeded when some old Franco generals tried a putsch in 1981.

The relative freedom African American soldiers experienced in Europe during and after World War II blazed one of the trails that led to the Civil Rights Movement in the 1950s. Rosa Parks, who in 1955 resisted sitting in the back of the bus in Montgomery Alabama, later became my personal heroine along with her namesake Rosa Luxemburg, pacifist and socialist before World War I in Germany who was murdered by Nationalist Guards. Her dead body was thrown into the *Landwehrkanal* in Berlin.

African American soldiers also fought in the World War I, the very war Rosa Luxemburg tried to convince German workers to resist. As I read in the *Journal of Negro History*, African American troops were used as "blood sponges" in the first line against William's Army, (Wilhelm II, emperor of Germany until World War I).

While my mother was struggling in 1946, taking care of her three children in the *Ostzone*, the Soviet Zone of Germany, my father was working in Ischlowsk in the Urals in the Soviet Union as prisoner of war. The German Soviet-occupied Eastern Zone had much more to pay for the wrongs of Nazi- Germany than the Western Zones-American-British-French-even though the horror of Nazi-Germany can never be repaid.

The Soviet Union had been destroyed and devastated by Germany in the war, now 1945 and later had train-and railway systems, whole factories and industries dismantled and reinstalled in many parts of Russia, also in the area of Ischlowsk where my father worked in the delousing ward underground. As a young adult I questioned my father.

He told me he was too weak to install railways above as other prisoners of war had to do during icy cold winters and hot summers. Even down there he became weaker and weaker, and finally with the help of a Jewish woman doctor he was sent home after a check-up "before he was going to die there," she told him. How much human strength and grace this woman must have had after what had been done to her people by Germans!

Sitting on top of a nut tree in our backyard on November 1946, my sister shouted to our mother, "There is a foreign man in our yard." When our father arrived back home from prisoner of war camp in Russia, thin and ragged, we did not recognize him. He was only skin and bones as my mother told me later. At the age of three I had to get used to a father, since I was only one year old when he had left. My father was lucky, many prisoners of war came home much later, the last ones in 1955, and some of them could not find their families. Many had died in the bombing or during the refugee track. Marriages ended after the homecoming because the partners and children had become estranged.

At that time, in 1947, my mother worked as a telephone operator to feed her three children while an older woman, Toska, kept an eye on us when we were not in kindergarten or in school. Toska was rather strict and sometimes spanked us since he had no knowledge of small children whatsoever. My father could not find work because he was too fragile and too near-sighted to work at construction sites; the Socialist Regime in East Germany wanted to change the working code of former intellectuals. Those who did brainwork before should do physical work now to give labourers the chance to study at universities.

In the 1930s my father had come from Berlin to work in the province where he met my mother who worked as a secretary under the same administration. My mother had to support her mother and grandmother after the worldwide economic crisis in 1929; they all lived in one house. My parents got married in the late 1930s and within five years they had three children. Mother stopped working to take care of us and our grandmother. Despite the War years my parents tried to create a happy childhood for us with walks in the park, flower picking in spring, sleigh rides in the winter, Christmas trees and candles and children's birthday parties.

Until 1944, when the last weak or almost blind men were drafted, my father had worked at the internal revenue service as a lawyer. After his law studies he had renounced to become an attorney or a judge, because he was aware under what circumstances he would have had to administer justice Even though he and his whole regional internal revenue office of about 120 employees were jointly inscribed as party members if they wanted or not. So my father had tried to avoid personal guilt, but in the end he could not resist. He was not in the German Resistance as I wished my father had been. But who am I to judge? What would I or everyone else have done under this regime being a young family of five? I wish I would have had the strength to resist, but who knows for sure? When I was between 15 and 30 I did not pose this kind of wise questions, I had attacked my father and his generation in many heartbreaking discussions as had done many of my friends. The arguments always went this way: In the beginning we thought the *Weimarer Republik* would soon put an end to this Spuk, to these strange happenings of the rabble rousers. People were following Hitler because they were still suffering from the end of World War I's Treaty of Versailles and the worldwide crisis and then it was too late because they were surrounded by undercover members of the secret police. I went on questioning my father and his generation with: But in the beginning, and they were answering with: But, but …. Many of the educated people like my father admitted what went wrong that lead to unimaginable terror, but had too many excuses; my generation could not accept. We were despaired, stunned, and hurt by what our parents and grandparents had let happen, but more so what the real Nazis had done.

My sense of justice was also rebelling against the fact that Russians and Americans right away after the War tried to get real Nazis to work for their own space labs and program, as they did with the rocket specialists of *Penemünde*. These specialists who were on their way to develop terrible weapons for the Nazis, and who used knowingly forced Jewish concentration camp workers to work for them in underground construction sites under cruelly inhuman circumstances, were later even honoured publicly by the US Government and by the Soviet Union.

My father studied at the Humboldt *Universität* in Berlin in the 1920's; at the same place where W. E. B. Du Bois studied economics and social science 30 years earlier in 1892 to

1895. This was the time when Du Bois had become a friend of German culture, and especially German classical music.

In 1993 the librarian at UMass of the Du Bois Centre asked us, a group of students of the African American Department, whether we knew what had been the favourite music of Du Bois. The amused students, most of them between 18 and 22 years old, guessed jazz or jokingly rap. So the librarian played an old registration for us, an interview of Du Bois at his 90th birthday in 1958. In the interview he was asked about his favourite music and he sang for the journalists in German Beethoven's *Freude schöner Götterfunken, Tochter aus Elysium*. Most of the young people did not recognize what it was but I felt a sudden touch of homesickness.

In 1947 my sister and brother were sent to live with relatives in Sweden and experienced at the age of ten and seven years their own after–the-War-Odyssey. They were taken by an aunt to a children's home at the coast of the Baltic Sea to wait for their cross over to Sweden since many health tests had to be done before they could enter the country. The aunt had to leave; my sister and brother found themselves alone among hundreds of other children who were searching for their parents having been lost in post war turmoil or in the westward trail of refugees at the end of the war. Still until the late 1950s one could hear daily radio broadcasting of the Red Cross reading the missing person bulletin starting with *Gesucht wird…Alter…zuletzt gesehen in* …we are searching for, age, last seen in.

For lack of an explanation my siblings thought searching for their parents themselves before they could finally leave for Sweden where they were put again in quarantine because Sweden was afraid of diseases being brought into the country. Eventually there they had to learn Swedish and to get used to a new family life and a new school.

After having escaped from the Soviet Zone my father found work in his old profession again the American Zone in Frankfurt a. Main while my mother and I stayed behind in my her hometown; she did not want to leave. But she took great risks many times to illegally cross the *Grüne Grenze*, the green border without border guards in the *Harz* mountain into the *Britische* Zone, then to transit into the American Zone to see my father in Frankfurt a. Main. It was known that if the British caught illegal border crossers they handed them over to the Soviets to be put in jail.

After three years of being separated in 1950 we gathered again as a family in Frankfurt. My mother suffering gravely from homesickness, my brother not speaking German anymore, my sister only sufficiently, and, I was struggling in the first grade with another school system. We had a hard time finding our way back to a family life in an apartment we shared with two other families in a quarter of Frankfurt with still a lot of houses in ruins. Strange, lonesome, and shady characters were all over the streets of Frankfurt.

During that time we got used to seeing people of colour in town. At the age of seven I do not remember having heard any talk about that, since we were all strangers in a new international environment, and as time went by we did not notice anymore. Four years later we moved to Friedberg, a small town of 22,000 inhabitants, 30 km north of Frankfurt. There were a lot of American soldiers, home of the Third Armoured Division. Here too African American soldiers were commonplace around town; they were integrated in the American Army since the army played a role model for the American society concerning integration, health insurance and retirement systems. Teenagers and young women had to pay attention to their so-called reputation when befriending American soldiers, white or Black. But there were those who did not care, and many German-American families were created and left for the US, some came back, but many did not.

My personal encounter with African American history began when I was 12 years old. I cried bitterly over Harriet Beecher Stoves' *Uncle Tom's Cabin*; and then in school we saw a film Tony, the story about an African American baby girl whose mother is German and her father is African American, who left Germany without knowing about the child. The German mother abandoned the baby girl on the steps of a church because she was desperate and feared German racism.

In recent years many Afro Germans, coming into their old age, are still searching for their African American fathers in the US, fathers who did not know children were born from their relationship to German women or who left their children behind when they had to leave, not wanting their families back home to know they had an interracial baby.

Growing up as a teenager in West Germany in the late 1950s and early 1960s I listened to AFN Frankfurt, Stuttgart and Munich for the best music, Rock 'n' Roll singers like Little Richard, The Platters, Ray Charles, and others were our favourite performers. In 1958, I was15 years old, my friends and I almost went crazy when we saw pictures in the newspapers of Elvis Presley arriving by boat in Bremerhaven and then having been transferred by train to the Ray-Barracks into our town. We loved Rock 'n' Roll; and now the King of Rock was doing his military service in Friedberg! He and his father and friends had been renting an apartment in Bad Nauheim, a beautiful small town nearby with a spa-infrastructure, in a hotel Art-Nouveau style house from the turn of the century. We could see him quite often coming from duty in the Ray Barracks in his, if I remember correctly, pink Cadillac "rolling" along broad *Kaiserstraße*, the main street of Friedberg, unusually broad for a medieval town with houses some of them more than 500 years old.

Years later during my continuing American and English studies in the early 1990s, I read Alice Walker's short story "1955" from her collection of short stories *You Can't Keep a Good Woman Down*. The character of the young man, Traynor, and whites claimed Black music as their own and the myth around Elvis leave the true originators without due recognition. I read in one issue of *Callaloo* that "1955" is discussed as white appropriation of Black authenticity and culture by white music industry and that Elvis is but one example. It is also said that behind this white singing of Black music there is no spiritual reality or that white performers and audience search for their own lost or repressed African or

Native American parts of themselves since they had lived together in the South for centuries.

Listening to AFN radio station daily, and babysitting for American army families in Friedberg, Black and whites helped me with my English in school and mastering the simple everyday English. Thus, I had the advantage to circumscribe difficult matters in the interpretation of British and American literature in school. James Baldwin's *Go Tell It On The Mountain* was my first encounter with African American literature.

In 1962, our girls' high school organized a Jazz Band-ball and as it came to *Damenwahl*/ladies choice, I walked over to the band and asked the African American saxophonist to dance with me. I was too excited to recognize the strange looks some of the students and teachers gave me, as told to me afterwards by my best friend. But nobody dared to say a word; and among students I had more admirers than critics. I was known as a kind of rebel, since I wore jeans to school, at that time not the proper way to dress in school. Some of us haunted history and social studies teachers by asking daring questions about German society of the time. Sitting around in cafes in all parts of the town we tried to show our disdain for the establishment, and did not care what people thought of or talked about us.

At home we had no television, as most people did not have, but I was excited by the radio news of boycotts and marches of the Civil Rights Movement in the US. The pictures were brought to us via the *Wochenschau*, the newsreel before the start of a film in the cinema. We went to the cinema at least three times a week and loved to see Sidney Portier and Sammy Davis Jr.

Nineteen sixty three had been a meaningful year for me, personally, politically and even historically, the year I finished high school with the German *Abitur*, a kind of baccalaureate and admission to university. I was enchanted to see President Kennedy and the cheerful crowd June 25th on the historical Frankfurt *Römer*, the place in front of the Frankfurt town hall, the crowning site of many kings and emperors until the 18th century. Later, in the 19th century, the *Römer* was also the gathering place for revolutionary crowds. Afterwards Kennedy gave a speech in the historical *Paulskirche* nearby where the first German Parliament came together in 1848, but unfortunately did not at that time, succeed in changing the German System of Government into a more democratic one. Kennedy's appearance in the *Paulskirche* was only a few days before his famous speech in West Berlin, where he expressed his solidarity with the people of Berlin in saying *Ich bin ein Berliner*. The people of West Berlin comprised of the French, British, and American Zones had been separated from the people of East Berlin, in the Soviet Zone.

The Berlin Wall had been built by the East German Government in 1961 to hinder East Germans from leaving the GDR, the German Democratic Republic via West Berlin and then taking the plane to West Germany. Not only citizens had been separated but families, relatives and friends. Additionally West Berlin had had been surrounded by the GDR and unimaginable bureaucratic efforts were necessary to visit family in East Berlin or East Germany if at all possible. West Berliner had to cross two borders to go on vacation in West Germany, and found themselves harassed by East German border controls, waiting for hours and being checked to cross the border into East Germany and into West Germany. The three Western powers had to negotiate again and again insisting on the so-called Four-Power-Agreement that guaranteed free access into and out of West Berlin for the people of West Berlin. The people of East Berlin did not have this freedom. Thus President Kennedy's *"Ich bin ein Berliner,"* more than welcomed by the crowd in front of the *Schöneberger Rathaus*, the city hall of West Berlin. They cheered and hailed President Kennedy as guarantor of their personal freedom.

In the US it was the year of racial unrest and civil rights demonstrations. My friends and I were praying, finally something is going to change. We believed in the principle of civil disobedience against injustice as Martin Luther King proclaimed it. In 1968 King became our role model to protest against the established German society and against the Vietnam War. The culmination of the civil rights protest I watched on American television while visiting my sister and family in Tewksbury, Massachusetts, my first stay in the US connected to such an important and touching event; The March on Washington on August 28, one day after the death of W.E.B. Du Bois in Ghana. Never before was I so deeply moved by a speech as Martin Luther King's "I have a Dream" speech. King was known to have been influenced by Mahatma Ghandi and by the German theologian Paul

Tillich, a member of the famous *Frankfurter Schule*, who had been barred from his job after 1933 because of his opposition to the Nazis. He immigrated to the United States after being invited to teach at the Union Theological Seminary. Tillich tried to combine his believe in an impersonal God with the philosophy of existentialism and socialism.

Back in Germany I started my studies at the *Universität* Frankfurter Main. During the winter semester we learned about the death of President Kennedy. We were as much shocked as the Americans and so sad that for the next weeks, my generation could only talk about this tragic event.

In 1966 I finished my exams at Frankfurter *Universität* to become a teacher. And at the same time Angela Davis did her philosophical and social studies at the so called Frankfurter *Schule*, a renowned institute of the philosophers Adorno and Horkheimer at Frankfurter *Universität*. Horkheimer and Adorno had founded the New School in New York City during their exile in the US from Nazi Germany, after the War they came back to their School in Frankfurt a. Main. I was proud to learn that Angela studied at my university since I felt connected to her critical mind.

In 1968 Angela Davis became part of the student revolution in Europe and in the US. Whether in France, Italy, Germany or the US, the young generation was questioning the politics of their parents, but in Germany this anti-society and anti-war movement had its very own questions. Student five years younger than me complained and rebelled against the fact that even 23 years after the World War II, Germans had not enough dealt with their recent past, and there were still some former Nazi-officials in the German Armed Forces, and in the German and Austrian Justice Administration, and medical research programs. In West and East Germany we hoped never again a war will take place with German participation.

A more profound insight into African American history, culture and literature I gained when in 1990 I took 3 years off my teaching job to continue studies at the Goethe *Universität* in Frankfurt a. Main, where I did my first studies in the 1960s. After basic literary studies I tried to combine African American, Caribbean and postcolonial studies, and thus the history of Africa and Europe and the Americas was constitutive for my understanding concerning this literature. My reading-canon contained among others Chinua Achebe, Maya Angelou, James Baldwin, Edward Brathwaite, Alejo Carpentiers, Michelle Cliff, Maryse Conde`, Henry Louis Gates, Langston Hughes, Zora Neale Hurston, Paule Marshall, Toni Morrison, V. S. Naipaul, Gloria Naylor, Jacques Roumain, Simone Schwarz-Bart, Wole Soyinka, Derek Walcott, Richard Wright, and as a base for it all we had to study literary and feminist theories.

A circle of intellectual interests cut into my lifetime socially and politically. My view on the world changed; and in the end I had the wonderful opportunity to study as a guest for one semester at the University of Massachusetts and Amherst College. Here, on February 27, I saw Angela Davis again giving an excellent speech on the occasion of 1993 Women's Conference at the University of Massachusetts.

She talked about her projects and experience having set up teaching programs in American prisons. She believes that there is no sense in jailing people without providing them an education, which will give them the opportunity to find a more positive sense in life. I had the impression of another circle cutting and closing, having had started in the 1960s when I admired Angela Davis' revolutionary impetus, and now the respect I felt for her intellectual and social work in American prisons and society.

In Amherst I was a stranger in the midst of another culture and geography, even if I was used to the country from so many visits to my sister, family and friends to Georgia, Florida, Virginia, Oregon, Massachusetts and Maine, I was still a long way from home. Questions occurred to me that had to do with my history and my culture. During the Holocaust Memorial Week I listened to reminiscences of children of Holocaust survivors; I felt sad and lonely. I was thrown back on my own national misery; since I am a politically determined person my own upbringing and personal history was once again questioned.

When I heard W.E.B. Du Bois singing the choir of Beethoven's Ninth Symphony I felt the obvious gap of the generations of students and theorists of African American Studies could not be wider and deeper. Memories of my father, who studied at the Humboldt *Universität* 30 years after Du Bois was in Berlin, sent back my thoughts to Germany. Du Bois' time in Berlin was not yet in the atmosphere of the pre-war national hysteria before 1914. Although in his autobiography, *A Soliloquy on Viewing My Life* he denounced German nationalism of the time, he underlined several times how much he enjoyed his two years in Germany. Compared to his studies at Harvard where he relished; but he felt at ease at Humboldt *Universität* in Berlin, in the company of his unconstrained contacts to students and professors, seen as an American student with academic interests and not so much as an exceptional Negro student. Already here I can see the beginning of his later psychological construct of 'Double Consciousness.'

Du Bois fell in love with a young German woman, the daughter of his host family in Eisenach where he had stayed several weeks before he started his studies in Berlin. Dora, the daughter of his host family, wanted to marry him, but he renounced considering his social status in the United States. I read his autobiography with historical interest, almost not believing what seemed possible at that time taking into consideration what kind of racism came into being in Germany later. At the Humboldt *Universität* he studied economics with Gustav Schmoller and Adolph Wagner; but mostly he worked with noted sociologist Max Weber. Around the same time German parties had been fighting for more democratic rights and eventually the imperial rule had to concede more rights to the German Parliament than before. Du Bois attended several times meetings of the Social Democratic Party that still exists today. The time before 1900 is also known as *Gründerjahre*, a period of flourishing industrial expansion in Germany from 1875 on, even the style of architecture in buildings and furniture reminds us today of the *Gründerzeit*.

When my father studied at the Humboldt *Universität* in the 1920s, there was again a sense of a new era about to dawn. The *Weimarer Republik* was the first real democratic system of government in Germany even if there were initial difficulties. The Roaring Twenties in Berlin and all over the world were known as a time of energetic enthusiasm and great tolerance in arts and lifestyle. My father told me about the activities of Nazi agitators were not yet to be seen or heard of in the university but they tried already their best to stir up poor people with their inflammatory speeches.

Without being conscious of this in Amherst, I looked and found many new revealing facts of my own country's history. While doing research on African American history in the library of U Mass in an ugly building with a high concrete pile, but with excellent library services, I tried to find answers to my questioning as to which African American authors and scholars went to segregated and non-segregated high schools from the 1930s to the 1960s and to what reading canon they were exposed to. So I interviewed scholars at the University such as Rhonda Cobham Sanders, Esther Terry, David Du Bois, Michael Thelwell and others. I read many issues of the *Journal of Negro History*, and found research analyses concerning my own country.

After World War I, from 1918 to 1928 parts of Western Germany had been occupied by the French Army, thus being part of the plan for reparations, Germany had to pay to France because of war damages done by Germans during the War. Agricultural products, coal, wood and steel, all being produced in the Rheinland and the Ruhrgebiet had to be transported to France under the surveillance of the French Army. Among the French soldiers were also Black soldiers from the so-called colonial troops. As it happens everywhere in the world there developed relationships with German young women and as a result interracial babies were born. Their fathers left or had to leave the country towards the end of occupation in 1929/30. Some of the Afro Germans today come from these families. Their parents were persecuted under the Nazis, and young males, if they were not hidden, were even forced to become sterilized.

Other Afro Germans come from relations between African American soldiers and German women after World War II, some of them were also from the Rheinland. Another circle is cutting into my existing one; I call them the second generation of Rhineland babies, now being between 40 and 60 years old and searching for their families in the US.

In the *Journal of Negro History*, I read complaints of African American families after World War II. The American Armed Forces Administration did not search as seriously for the fate of their missing soldiers as German prisoners of war, as they did for their white soldiers. But what was more interesting and saddening for me was the fact that Black prisoners of war were treated differently by the Nazis than their white comrades. The agreement of the Geneva Convention for prisoners of war was not applied to them as it was on white American prisoners of war. Black soldiers were often separated, more insulted and punished and less provided with medical help and food rations. That is not known and discussed in German society of today, although I know it is out there in some historical research reports.

But I was proud and content at how open the Frankfurter *Universität* was in the early 1990s regarding historical matters of Nazi times. Information was researched and discussed as well as European racism at universities throughout Europe in the 19th and 20th centuries. One circle cut into another as I could compare and connect my acquired knowledge in different departments of the university. At the department of educational science I participated in a seminar about the European transfer of educational systems into former colonies. My professor was Dr. Diaz. Together with the other students we concluded that he was Portuguese. But he told us the story of his name. In the 17th century the Portuguese sailed along the West Coast of India. Captain Diaz of the Portuguese vessel came on land and the natives gathered around him greeting him in a very friendly way. He answered in his friendly way, and that was now his land; all inhabitants his children and all were named Diaz. As one can imagine or not still today in this region there are many families with that name. The history of American enslavers came to my mind and how they renamed their enslaved individuals no matter what their authentic names were.

Another circle cut into the existing ones six years later in Paris when I studied French history and culture at the Sorbonne. The French professor talked to us about how the wonderful houses in Bordeaux and Nantes from the 18th century were built by the French bourgeois who wanted to compete with the French aristocracy. The money they built the houses with came from the exploitation of cruel slave labour in the French colonies of the West Indies.

I was so pleased that in Amherst, Frankfurt, and in Paris, the academia became self-critical and questioned the self-esteem of older generations of historians that refused to take into account the latest findings of historical research.

In 2003 I witnessed in Paris the reburial of Alexandre Dumas, the French author of the 19th century. All French school children have to and love to read his historical novels rather than dry history textbooks. He had been buried somewhere in the French province since he was of black Caribbean decent. Now to be honoured his casket was brought to the Senate in the *Jardin du Luxembourg* and from there in a carriage drawn by 2 white horses to the Pantheon. Torches were being lit by young actors dressed in costumes of Dumas' historical plays along the way. He was to be buried there next to his friend Victor Hugo another important French author of the 19th century. The French National Guard greeted the procession at the entrance of the Pantheon, and President Jacques Chirac gave a speech honouring Dumas. But most important, he apologized for the French nation having had participated in the Slave Trade. For me another circle cut. One can argue that it was just a show and racism still exists also in France. Partly, I would agree, but on the other hand, we need vision and symbols for a better world to come, to fight and overcome injustice. My German-African American-French Circle is complete.

Acknowledgments

I am deeply indebted to the many people who encouraged and supported me during this journey. Writing a book is a long and lonely process. I am thankful to have had friends and supporters willing to read and reread drafts; write letters for me to compete for fellowships, which gave me time to write and think; and others who believed I could complete this book with the passion I felt for it.

If I have left any names from this page, it is because of a lack of memory, not a lack of gratitude. Thank you: Gail Galloway Adams; Jeanetta Britt; Louise & Sev Bruyn; Kim Connor; Jimmy Cusack; Janice Eidus; Patricia Elam; Anna Elfenbein; John Ernest; Virginia Fowler; Nikki Giovanni; Marguerite Guzman-Bouvard; Patricia Hampl; Trudier Harris; Kaite Hillenbrand; Karla Holloway; Virginia Ingram; Kathy Jones; Lisa Jones; Andrea Lee; P⸱   ⸱⸱ N ⸱ters; Opal Moore; Marilyn Moriarty; Rc   ⸱; Joyce Pettis; Sara Pritchard; E⸱   Julia Shivers; Isabelle Shepherd⸱ Alvene Williams.

I am equally grateful to my German friends and colleagues: Rosemarie Abendroth; Donna Blagg; Bernd and Lucia Engler; Harmutt and Ursula Grandel; Martina Kohl; Silvia Kunze-Ritter; Klaus Ritter; Oliver and Christine Scheiding; Horst Tonn, Ulli Wagner; and all of the staff in American Studies at the Universität Tübingen; and the US Fulbright Commission. I further extend gratitude to: DAIs; Universitäts of Graz, Frankfurt, Rockstock, Berlin, Wittenberg, Cologne; Munich; Hamburg; US Embassies of Germany and Belgium; US Information Service; GAWC; and other institutions and organizations that hosted me.

I wish to acknowledge the support of West Virginia University's Eberly College of Arts & Sciences and the Department of English, where I have been a faculty member since 1993. I was also awarded support from: The Women's Studies Research Center at Brandeis University; the Rockefeller Foundation-Bellagio, Italy; the American Academy in Rome; the Virginia Center for the Creative Arts; my Sisters of the Wintergreen Collective; the Highland Park Tennis League of Pittsburgh; and the Connotation Press.

Getting to know friends and colleagues in Germany was an honor and a great joy. This work inspired and connected me to a world I couldn't have imagined possible. It is my hope that I am a bigger and better person from my journey, which I will always carry it with me.

About the Author

Ethel Morgan Smith is the author of *From Whence Cometh My Help: The African American Community at Hollins College*. Her essay "Love Means Nothing" was the winner of the Mid-Atlantic Arts Prize for Nonfiction. "Outside of Dreams" was recently published in *Shaping Memories: Reflections of African American Women Writers*. Her work has been published in: *The New York Times; Callaloo; African American Review; That Mintorithing*.com, and other national and international outlets.

Professor Smith has received the following awards: Fulbright-Tübingen, Germany; Rockefeller Foundation Fellowship-Bellagio, Italy; DuPont-Randolph-Macon Woman's College; American Academy in Rome-Visiting Artist; Women's Studies Research Center at Brandeis University; Bread Loaf; and Virginia Center for the Creative Arts. Professor Smith is Associate Professor of English at West Virginia University.